Access by Design

"What is accessibility? So many people don't realize what access means. To me, it means not going through garbage elevators, and not going through a garage, but going through a main door where everybody else goes. It means a spontaneity in lifestyle.

"I want to go buy my tickets. I don't want to go to a special place; I want to go to the box office.

"The question I get asked all the time by architects for concert halls is, 'How do I determine what would make a certain building physically accessible?' And I tell them, well, it's very simple, you put yourself in a wheelchair and go around 'til you cannot go any more. That means that spot is not accessible. It's very simple. There is no genius at work here.

"I know that nobody thinks twice about an exit sign in a concert hall so that people can escape in case of fire, and yet they have to think more than three times whether or not a ramp should go in. It should be a very natural thing.

"Next time you are on the sidewalk and you see a curb-cut, pay attention to how many people prefer using the cut versus the step. Everybody uses the curb-cut. To me, that is universal design."

—*Itzhak Perlman*
Musician

*Excerpted from "Universal Design: Access to Daily Living" Conference, *Interior Design* Magazine

Access by Design

George A. Covington

Bruce Hannah

VAN NOSTRAND REINHOLD

I(T)P® A Division of International Thomson Publishing Inc.

New York · Albany · Bonn · Boston · Detroit · London · Madrid · Melbourne
Mexico City · Paris · San Francisco · Singapore · Tokyo · Toronto

Cover photos courtesy of (top row-left to right) Motorola, Inc.; Playworld Systems; Toto Ltd.; (middle row) JCDecaux; Timex; Microsoft Corp.; (bottom row) Biomorph; Herman Miller; Yashica Optical Division, Kyocera Electronics, Inc.
Cover Design: Mike Suh

Van Nostrand Reinhold Staff
Editor: Jane Degenhardt
Production Editor: Carla Nessler

Production Manager: Mary McCartney
Interior Designer: Paul Costello

Copyright © 1997 by George Covington and Bruce Hannah
I(T)P® A division of International Thomson Publishing Inc.
The ITP logo is a registered trademark under license

Printed in the United States of America
For more information, contact:

Van Nostrand Reinhold
115 Fifth Avenue
New York, NY 10003

Chapman & Hall
2-6 Boundary Row
London
SE1 8HN
United Kingdom

Thomas Nelson Australia
102 Dodds Street
South Melbourne, 3205
Victoria, Australia

Nelson Canada
1120 Birchmount Road
Scarborough, Ontario
Canada M1K 5G4

Chapman & Hall GmbH
Pappelallee 3
69469 Weinheim
Germany

International Thomson Publishing Asia
221 Henderson Road #05-10
Henderson Building
Singapore 0315

International Thomson Publishing Japan
Hirakawacho Kyowa Building, 3F
2-2-1 Hirakawacho
Chiyoda-ku, 102 Tokyo
Japan

International Thomson Editores
Seneca 53
Col. Polanco
11560 Mexico D.F. Mexico

2   3   4   5   6   7   8   9   10   COU-WF   03   02   01   99   98   97

Library of Congress Cataloging-in-Publication Data
Covington, George.
    Access by design / George Covington & Bruce Hannah.
        p.   cm.
    Includes bibliographical references and index.
    ISBN 0-442-02126-7
    1. Architecture and the physically handicapped—United States.
  I. Covington, George.   II. Title.
    NA2545.P5H36   1996
    720'.42'0973—dc20   96-3175
                                                                CIP

http://www.vnr.com
product discounts • free email newsletters
software demos • online resources
email: info@vnr.com   A service of I(T)P®

CONTENTS

Foreword

Preface: A Review of Universal Products

DEDICATION

I would like to dedicate my portion of this book to the memory of my mother Stella Davis Purifoy (1923–1995), and also to two remarkable women: Ruth Majbritt Fireman and Karen Fireman.

Last, but not least, RitaSue Siegel, the best design headhunter on the planet.

—*George Covington*

I would like to dedicate my portion of this book to my wife Nancy and my daughters Rebekah and Elizabeth.

—*Bruce Hannah*

A portion of the proceeds for this book will be dedicated to the Universal Design Scholarship Fund, Cooper-Hewitt National Design Museum, Smithsonian Institution.

ACKNOWLEDGMENTS

The authors would like to thank Linda Lee, without whom this book wouldn't exist; Danae Loran Wilson, of Pratt Institute, who helped compile the bibliography; Jane Saks-Cohn, who started the Universal Design Archive at CADRE Pratt Institute, Brooklyn, NY; RitaSue Siegel, who contributed time and energy; and Kim Beasley/Paradigm Design Group and Paralyzed Veterans of America, who continue to break new ground for a barrier-free society. We would also like to thank the manufacturers and designers who freely contributed their time, energy, and work, and to the hundreds of people who work diligently to make the world a little more accessible each day—thank you also.

FOREWORD

Why should we spend all this money to comply with the Americans with Disabilities Act (ADA) for a handful of people? First of all, 49 million is not exactly a small number. But that is not the point. The ADA is not just for the disabled; it is for all of us. Designers generally tend to design for a limited number of people—right-handed individuals of a certain height and weight, between the ages of 18 and 55. These individuals do not have arthritis, or back pain, or broken ankles. They do not have children and they never age. At best, this description covers only a small fraction of the population. That is why the ADA and Universal Design—designing for the majority, not the minority—are so important.

Before I used a wheelchair, my knowledge of accessibility and Universal Design was rudimentary. However, once I was in a wheelchair, I quickly and painfully learned the true meaning of accessibility. I was handicapped by only one thing—the design of the built environment. It disturbs me that facilities that claim to be accessible are often not, even though considerable amounts of money have been spent on accessible improvements. Clearly many people view the ADA as just another annoying set of government regulations that do not have any bearing on their lives. This means, unfortunately, that little thought is given to whether the accessibility improvements actually correct the problem or are even attractive. Why not view compliance with the ADA as a way to serve more people, create new business opportunities, open new markets for products, and, in the process, make more money?

Accessibility and Universal Design are real issues of creative problem solving, the very definition of "good" design. Design must be functional, aesthetic, adaptable, democratic, environmentally sensitive, and economically viable for both manufacturer and consumer. By using the concept of Universal Design, designers have the ability—and the responsibility—to create a better world for everyone.

Dianne Pilgrim
Director, National Design Museum

PREFACE

Access by Design is a review of Universal Products: Universal Design is for the elderly, the disabled, and the young-old—the Baby Boomers.

Accommodating as many people as possible as they pursue the activities of daily life is the goal of Universal Design. From the moment we wake in our homes until we return to bed at night, design has an effect on the way we access and use spaces, products, and services. Design can help or hinder these activities. This book highlights many of the better solutions to universal access and Universal Design.

Each of the chapters presents solutions from spaces, to products—then services the assumption since 50 percent of any solution is determining how the space will be used and the other 50 percent is in the details. The efficient design of space depends on an understanding of the products and services to be used in that space. As an example, The Home and Living chapter starts with solutions to the bath and kitchen and access to them and continues with products that accommodate activities in these spaces and then services. Highlighted at the beginning of each chapter is the product, service, or space that is most universal in design and use and is used as an example for the critique of that chapter. They set the tone and give a goal to pursue. We tried to keep in mind that style, elegance, and beauty are not universals but value systems that are determined by the buyer and beholder. The end of the chapter is devoted to conceptual work in areas that are not covered by the existing spaces, products, or services which present solutions and concepts that are not necessarily presently possible but are goals to be approached.

The goal of Universal Design is to create a product, place, or service that can be used by the widest possible range of individuals. If the product, place, or service can be used by both an individual who is eight years old and a person who is 80 years old, you are close to reaching the goal of Universal Design. Within this eight-to-80 range most, but not all, disabled people will fit. Designs and designers who strive to meet this goal of Universal Design are the subjects covered in the text. By reviewing and evaluating certain spaces, products, and services that approach the concept of Universal Design, we provide an overview and introduction to this new field. The book must, in itself, represent good accessible design. It must be accessible to as wide an audience as possible. It is printed in high-contrast, 14 point ITC Legacy Sans type with adequate spacing to maximize reading ease. **The impact Universal Design has had on the design of the home, workplace, transportation, communications, computers, furniture, products, and services is the subject of this book.** From kitchen tools to computers, Universal Designs are finding a wide audience that has discovered the ease, convenience, and safety that the designs encompass. As the home becomes more like the office and the office more like home a universality is creeping into our daily lives whether we like it or not. Computers are daily making accessibility a watchword.

As new markets emerge designers have the choice of either putting everyone in a niche or designing universally. Global competition is the opposite of niche marketing. Universal Design looks at a product from the broadest possible usage and, thus, at its widest marketing potential. The emerging world markets will demand better-designed, safer, and longer-lasting products, Universal Design provides some answers to the direction design might take.

Writing a book that bills itself as a Universal Design Review is probably presumptuous at best and arrogant at its worst, but we tried. Maybe there are a few things in here you haven't seen before or a few thoughts you haven't heard before. This is a start in trying to define how designers might help reshape the world for universal access.

George Covington
Bruce Hannah

CHAPTER 1

INTRODUCTION

Transitions

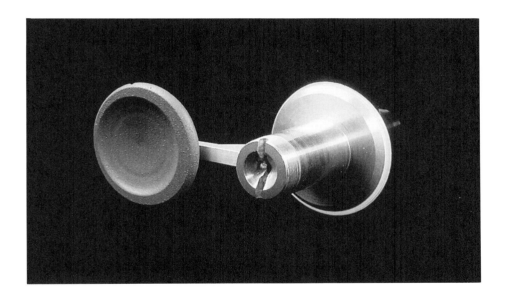

Figure 1.1 **Door Handle. (*See Figure 3.19*) (*Courtesy of Lutz Savant, Pratt Institute*)**

The most interesting times, places, and occurrences are transitions. Birth, adolescence, marriage, divorce, and death are the times of a life that are the most traumatic, joyful, stressful, or delightful. The most interesting design problems also occur at transitions. Column-to-beam transitions define our understanding of Ionic, Doric, and Corinthian. The transitory nature of these periods is expressed in the design of the transition between column and beam, but the basic structure remains constant. The Gothic cathedral attempts to make the transition from vertical (column) to horizontal (beam) seamless. The Gothic cathedral structure is the embodiment of transition, both physically and metaphorically, of the thirteenth century. Look at any structure, no matter how big or small, and the only place anything of significance takes place is at a transition. Whether it is a spoon's transition from bowl to handle (decoration), a wall's transition to a ceiling (crown molding), or a road's transition to sidewalk (curb), designs, styles, and structures happen at transitions. The rest of the time it's pretty quiet.

Universal Design problems occur at transitions. Curbs on sidewalks presented a major obstacle for the disabled until a transition was designed; a curb cut. Now everyone benefits from the curb cut, especially parents pushing strollers, delivery people, and, of course, the disabled. Transitions from light to dark, from inside to outside, from upstairs to downstairs, all present design problems that can be solved universally. Establishing the design parameters at transitions can lead to universal solutions. Recognizing that the aging population begins to lose sight acuity around 40 years of age can help define ground rules concerning how floors change at entrances and exits to announce the entering or exiting of a space.

"Announcing" the edge of a counter, shelf, floor, deck, or stair as a transition helps everyone to make a passage from one space or area to another. Or helps someone keep objects or work on the counter, shelf, or desktop. An edge, of contrasting color, that is raised on counters and shelves helps define and clarify the area of work.

The concept of **Universal Design** is best understood in the area of transitions. A product, service, or place, when universally designed, is not an isolated island but a transition. An employer, facilities manager, or office supervisor must understand that they can look beyond one narrow goal and understand the broader and continuing aspects of Universal Design's role in seamlessly integrating individuals into all aspects of our culture.

All doors are transitions from inside to outside, whether in autos, homes, or buildings. The transitions from inside to outside, from up to down, from light to dark, from open to closed, from on to off, from top to bottom, from young to old can be universal and easy for everyone if **everyone** is considered from the beginning.

As we make life transitions from child to teen to adult to parent to grandparent, we also gain and lose physical and mental acuity. This is called **aging.** Universal Design's goal is to make the transitions of life and the transitions in design as elegant as possible.

Bruce Hannah

The Trojan Horse of Design

The concept of Universal Design as a Trojan Horse will allow people with disabilities past the gates of prejudice and fear. By understanding Universal Design from a disability perspective, it is also a concept that can broaden domestic markets and aid this country in global competition.

The goal of Universal Design is to create a product, place, or service that can be used by the widest range of individuals possible. If the product, place, or service can be used by both a person who is eight years old and a person who is 80 years old, you are close to reaching the goal of Universal Design. Within this eight-to-80 range most, but not all, disabled people will fit.

Universal Design is intended to be **in**clusive not **ex**clusive. The concept's inclusive nature allows disabled people to fit within the Trojan Horse.

Why do America's 49 million Americans need a Trojan Horse?

Because designers are people and people fear us.

In 1991, a Louis Harris Poll showed that 58% of able-bodied persons interviewed felt embarrassed and uncomfortable in the presence of a person with a disability, and 47% felt actual **fear.** If you fear us, how can you design for us?

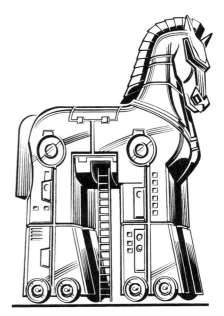

Figure 1.2 **Trojan Horse.**

To get past the fear you must understand that we are not one mass of creatures called "the disabled." Designers must understand that disabled people are just like everyone else, except we have a disability. Our individual disability becomes a handicap **only** when we encounter structural or attitudinal barriers. Designers, not God, created most of the barriers we face. Ramping a building is easier than ramping the human heart and mind. We can't change God, but we can definitely change designers by destroying the fear.

To get past the fear, you have to get past the negative images, the stereotypes, and the myths. It will help if you consider a few facts and take some simple advice.

The first fact is: People with disabilities can lie, cheat, and steal just like able-bodied people. Disabled people can be fools, fakes, and frauds just like able-bodied people. If you cannot accept these statements, you cannot truly accept the concept that disabled people are just like everyone else, except they have a disability.

Some of us with disabilities are charming, witty, and highly intelligent; some of us are not. The disability didn't determine which of us would be **sexy** and which of us would be **sexist.** A disability gives us a different perspective, not a different personality.

Some of us get married, have children, live happily ever after, and some of us get divorced (not necessarily in that order). Some of us never leave home; most of us do.

Some of us have reached a comfort level that allows us to debate semantics and determine that "cripple" and "handicapped" are no longer acceptable. Others are still debating whether "disabled people" should be replaced with "people with disabilities." This latter debate is generally restricted to the disabled gurus living inside the Washington, D.C. Beltway. Yes, some of us are disabled gurus, or gurus with disabilities, if you choose. Many of us feel that we are not "visually challenged," "physically challenged," or, if you're short, "vertically challenged." When the obstacles are removed so are the "challenges."

If designers will stop creating a world of barriers that constantly "challenge" us, we poor crips will stop "inspiring" people with how we manage to overcome the challenge of the bad designs.

We are as different and diverse as everyone else in the world. We simply have a disability.

The second fact is: "The road to Hell is paved with good intentions." Most designers have approached disability issues with the best of intentions, but good intentions are not enough.

Too often in the past, able-bodied individuals and groups came up with projects and products that they **knew** "would be great for handicapped people." They just never bothered to ask us for our input. Their enthusiasm was great, but their idea or product was a disaster. They were more interested in a "warm and fuzzy, feel-good" concept than they were in a substantive idea. Often their feelings were hurt when we threw the cold water of reality on what had been the warm glow of poorly directed good intentions. It is too late to ask for our input after the concrete has been poured and the last nail driven. Tens of millions of dollars have been wasted on projects for disabled people. Able-bodied people must learn to ask us if we need it, want it, or can afford it. **Ask** us. Then **listen.** Then **design.**

And don't listen to just one of us. Most designers we know would seek input from as many potential consumers as possible before finishing a design and taking it to market. Please avoid the "I-have-this-disabled-friend" syndrome. It sometimes appears that everyone in the design business has one disabled person who can provide all necessary knowledge on all aspects of disability.

A Fortune 500 company once asked coauthor George Covington's opinion of a new product they were getting ready to market.

"**Why the hell they wanted my input after** they had finished the design was not clear, but a free meal is a free meal.

"Considering the limitations of the technology at the time, the overall design was good.

" 'Why did you select such dull colors for the housing and why didn't you color code your keyboard?' I asked.

"There was silence.

" 'I know you are aware that 90 percent of your potential market will be people who are legally blind but have usable sight. We semiblinds like color."

"Silence.

" 'Did you consult with any disabled people on the project?'

" 'Yes!' my four able-bodied dinner companions said in unison. 'We talked to Melvin every step of the way and **he's** blind.'

" 'Has he been totally blind since birth?

" 'Yes!'

" 'Did it ever dawn on you that he has never seen a color and would have no concept of using color as a code? You asked one blind person to advise you on a product that will be used by sighted people composing 90 percent of your potential market?' "

"I didn't get desert.

"This mentality is the same as saying, 'They all look alike to me.'

"Well, look again. The latest government figures show there are 49 million of us and the numbers are growing as the population ages. As America grays, so does its purses and pocketbooks."

As the Baby Boomers hit the brick wall of 50, many are not seeing, hearing, or moving as well as they did in their youth. Because of the stigma attached to the term **disabled,** these newcomers will seldom discuss their problems. Because they have believed the negative images, myths, and stereotypes of "the disabled," they are horrified that they might be one of us.

These newcomers to the fringes of disability bring with them the fear of "the disabled." Often, if the problem is severe, these individuals will retreat within the safety of their homes and seldom venture out. They will choose being a hermit over the stigma of being disabled. The Trojan Horse of Universal Design can get through the walls these people have erected from myths and stereotypes.

How?

By designing something for as broad a market as possible, a design is no longer "special" and no longer identifies the user as different and apart from everyone else.

For example, a situation where a museum would place a pile of attractive large-print brochures next to a "regular" small-print brochure. If they placed a sign "for the handicapped," the stack will stay untouched until it turns moldy. Take away any designation of the two stacks and you can watch the "regular" stack turn old and gray. Why do so many able-bodied folks use those things designed for us when they aren't aware of that fact? Because they want the convenience of an accessibly designed creation without the perceived stigma.

Universal Design is, at its best, seamless and invisible. You don't look at something and say "that's designed for. . . ."

Universal Design does not mean that **all** people will be able to use the end product. Some severely disabled individuals will need specific modification for use. With Universal Design, however, fewer and less-costly modifications will be needed.

The Trojan Horse of Universal Design will allow these newcomers to use products, places, and services they might otherwise avoid.

George Covington

CHAPTER 2

OTHER THOUGHTS ON UNIVERSAL DESIGN

Emerging Markets: Merging Markets

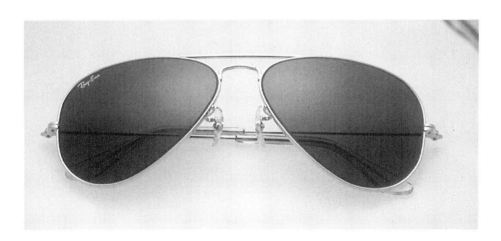

Figure 2.1 **Ray-Ban Classics Sunglasses. (*Courtesy of Bausch & Lomb.*)**

Three emerging markets—the "Baby Boomers," who are the young to early middle aged, "the Disabled," and "the Elderly"—will demand designs that are universal in their approach. Design that is accessible; Design that allows them to lead full productive and independent lives; Design that is both beautiful and functional. Products, services, and places that are universally designed will be used, purchased, and accessed by this huge audience. Architecture that is accessible, services that are deliverable, and products that are usable can command an audience of 70 million people. America's Baby Boomers make up the richest market ever.

As years pass, the lines have begun to blur and will continue to blur, so the Baby Boomers, the Disabled, and the Elderly merge into one enormous market for Universal Design. The Baby Boomers passing the half-century mark are a market worth in excess of $200 billion. They are willing to pay—and pay well—to overcome their slight diminution of sight, hearing, and movement and for the conveniences that make their lives easier.

As time goes on, we are discovering that the end of the Baby Boomer era marks a decline in the pool of workers available. To avoid a bidding war, and thus increase inflation, many of the middle- and upper-level managers must be convinced to remain in the job market. Companies must maximize the potential of their older workers if they are going to maintain their competitive edge by retaining their experienced personnel. Universal Design will help maintain this level of experience and maintain their level of productivity.

More than $200 billion a year is spent at the local, state, and national levels on the disability community and related issues.

Intention

Designers are constantly looking for ways to challenge the ideas of design. How do we look for new ideas, and how do we establish criteria, definitions, and goals so that we can develop ideas that are generally useful? If we look at the history of invention, we find that most of the important and extraordinary inventions occurred, not because people were looking for them, but because they were determined to solve a problem which, to them, was extraordinary. The invention of the telephone occurred because Alexander Graham Bell was attempting to create a hearing aid; the

Figure 2.2 **Motorola's Microtac** (*See Figure 7.1*) (*Courtesy of Motorola, Inc.*)

typewriter became a tool for the blind to communicate effectively; the lens as a way to aid sight, leading to the invention of the microscope, telescope, etc. As simple a concept as the football huddle was arrived at when one signing school played another, so that the opposition could not see them signing!

All of these inventions have two threads running through them: the concept of communication, as discussed in Chapter 1, and the idea of microcosm. These inventions happened by not generalizing or looking for a common denominator, but by focusing on a small **problem** and a small **solution.** By attempting to solve the problems for small populations we might stumble onto products that are not obvious at first but are general solutions to generalized problems.

There are disabled people in the workplace, some temporarily disabled, some disabled for a lifetime. Statistically, they are significant, but seldom represented or discussed when office products are designed. A disability can mean not only the obvious (e.g. a wheelchair user), but also arthritis, nerve disorders, etc. Therefore, this area of investigation could include not only furniture but all the instruments of the office. If the work areas of the disabled in the office were explored, some very interesting problems and their resultant solutions might come to light.

The telephone is a terrific hearing aid; in fact we can hear Tokyo from New York very clearly. Did Alexander Graham Bell in his wildest dreams believe that communication would be so immediate or as easy as the personal flip phone makes it? Is there a solution to mobility that we have overlooked because we are searching in too wide an area and not looking in a small, well-defined population?

There are abstract solutions to problems, but we may be looking for them in the wrong way. By designing intentionally for small, defined populations, large abstract solutions might happen.

Figure 2.3 **Apple Computer.** (*Courtesy of Apple Computer, Inc.*)

Technology—A Two-Edged Sword

"I have had a lot of help with this book from Brian Whitt, one of my students. I caught pneumonia in 1985, after I had written my first draft. I had to have a tracheotomy operation which removed my ability to speak, and made it almost impossible for me to communicate. I thought I would be unable to finish it. However, Brian not only helped me revise it, he also got me using a communications program, called "Living Center," which was donated to me by Walt Woltosz, of Words Plus, Inc., in Sunnyvale, California. With this I can both write books and papers and speak to people using a Speech Synthesizer donated by Speech Plus, also of Sunnyvale, California. The Synthesizer and a small personal computer were mounted on my wheelchair by David Mason. This system had made all the difference. **In fact I can communicate better now than before I lost my voice!**"

Stephen Hawking, 20th October 1987
Lucasian Professor of Mathematics at Cambridge University
From: A Brief History Of Time

Technology has replaced the physical skills necessary for design communication. Fifty years ago this was unthinkable and it is still considered heresy today to encourage potential designers without physical skills to participate in the process of design. The collective value judgment concerning skills has most certainly discouraged many potential designers from participating in design. Design is not a skill-based profession, however. It requires recognizing problems, small or large, in existing products and finding (and designing) a solution. Usually, the people best "equipped" to find solutions are those who must otherwise cope with the problems. Broadening the avenues into design professions allows individuals with disabilities to design.

Although technology allowed Hawking to continue to contribute to the scientific community, it can be a two-edged sword. The technology that has helped millions of disabled people adjust can just as easily create misconceptions that can hinder their progress to the so-called "mainstream." Too often people will assume that technology alone will allow a person to fulfill an assigned task in an office, without giving any thought to how a person gets to the office, gets past a curb, finds the building, or even how to get into the office door. A $5000 investment in state-of-the-art technology is worthless if the person can't independently reach the technology.

Too narrow a view of Universal Design and technology can easily put many disabled and aging individuals back into society's backroom. The easiest cop-out is to use telecommuting as an excuse for individuals to remain at home, thus allowing site managers to disregard all aspects of access to facilities. Social interaction is too important to be sacrificed on the alter of expediency.

The Nature of Universal Design

Universal Design is intended to be inclusive not exclusive. Universal Design is the idea that **everyone should have access to everything all of the time,** a difficult-but-not-

Figure 2.4 **Barrier-Free Home by Jane Langmuir. (*See Figure 3.12 Living Area*). (*Courtesy of David Lund.*)**

impossible task if products, architecture, and services are thought of universally from the start; if there is an inclusiveness right from the beginning.

Politics, economics, and education are both inherent obstacles and inherent allies right from the inception of an idea. Politically, the idea of **inclusiveness** is not new. Economically, **inclusiveness** reeks of increased cost because people see access as something they don't have to think about and don't have to do unless coerced by laws. Education has proven to be both a powerful ally and foe. Education has helped people to understand that we are no less similar to anyone else and we should be no more separated or defined by our disability than should a person by hair color or height. Architecture and design curriculums, however, do not include it as a component of the syllabus. "Universal Design" is treated separately as "Human Factors," "Ergonomics," or some other scientific issue. Universal Design is not a separate issue, it is **the** issue. Universal Design can tie a whole curriculum together, it can humanize the education of young people, it can make design reasonable. Universal Design is **design with reason.**

Everything designers make or build is a **prosthesis.** Flying on an airplane is a terrific replacement for the feathers we don't have. Riding in a cab or bus is much easy and faster than walking home from the airport. These are designs/concepts with reasons.

These are really Universal Designs—created to be at the disposal of everyone to make their lives easier. Can every person use every Universal Design? Of course not. Some things have to be modified for use—for all sorts of people, not just those with disabilities. For example, some buses have "kneeling" stairs, which lower to make it easier for children and the elderly to step on.

Designers have been very exclusive about who they design for, the statistical "norm"; Joe & Josephine Smith, both perfect in their entirety. Joe & Josephine never aged, never got fat, never tired, never varied in their daily discipline. In fact they never missed a beat.

Who were they?

They were no one. They were usually faceless, odorless, crash dummies! They weren't **anyone!**

Universal Design is creating scenarios of people with gender, faces, and personality and design for real people, whoever they might be. Designers can no longer design for norms because there aren't any! They must design for the many, not the few.

Universal Design is about designing for, and supporting, people—people with real names. Everyone from the child named Sylvia to the grandfather named Matt. Putting a real person into the picture permits reaction to the designer's action. **Universal Design** is transgenerational design—design for grandfather as well as for grandchild. It is **not** designing solely within the vacuum of self!

Universal Design is a Way of Life

Universal Design supports the activities of daily living and tries to meet the needs of as large an audience as possible

Figure 2.5 **Adjustable Chair Parachute by Knoll** *(See Figure 4.51.)* **Designed by Dragomir Ivicevic of the Knoll Group.**

by designing inclusively not exclusively. This is done by designing with all the senses—sight, sound, touch, smell, taste, and kinesthetics (the sense of where we are in space)—not just one or two senses, all of the time. The senses are underutilized as individual message centers. Designers have to start using them as media coordinators.

Elevators, for example, are very universal: the use of sight, with backlit buttons; sound, with the bells announcing each floor; touch, with braille identifying the control and floor button.

Action words, or **gerunds,** are verbs that describe actions, such as walking; talking; sleeping; writing; bathing; typing; drawing; sketching; riding; cooking; driving; skiing; swimming; jumping; dancing; playing; thinking; and just plain **being**—the-**ing** words. Designers should be aware that their designs support the activities of daily living.

Design Sense or Nonsense

Designers must become acutely aware of the six senses that are available to facilitate the interaction between a product a place or a service. But think how most products are described or **seen.** Usually we as a society judge everything by its looks! How we **perceive** it, not how it is used. Designers need to start **seeing** the world as others see it, or **don't** see

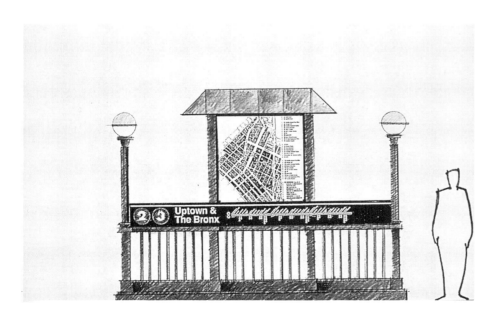

Figure 2.6 **NY Transit #10** (*See Figure 8.21*) (*Courtesy NY Transit.*)

it. Acutely visually impaired people don't **see** the world; they **hear** it, **feel** it, and **touch** it. That is their way of getting around, using, and interacting. As designers we must begin to understand the way products, services, and places **communicate** with the world at large. Using the senses of sight, touch, smell, sound, taste, and kinesthetics redundantly can enhance the use of everything for everyone. A subway that announces both its arrival and present time and identifies itself and its destination not only provides a visually impaired person with information but **everyone** with enhanced information.

Back to the future—all of this information was provided years ago by a **conductor,** a **person,** but that is economically unfeasible. A microchip can be utilized to make the same announcements. The redundancy of information will make it safer and more convenient to ride the subway.

Accessibility, Responsibility, and Communication—A Design Agenda for the '90s

Bruce Hannah has been a part-time educator for 25 years and a full-time one for the last six years: "I have had to come to terms with the struggle of dealing with "old" design agendas. Namely, Modernism, Post Modernism, and assorted short-lived ones from Memphis to Semantics. Over the last decade a few ideas have been rising from the murky depths of design symposiums and governments. Much-discussed and much-maligned terms, like social responsibility, accessibility, ecology, and education are being discussed as part of a new design agenda."

Where it was once enough to make buildings, interiors, furniture, and objects aesthetically acceptable, ergonomically comfortable, and socially acceptable for the elite, the healthy, and exclusively "able," it isn't anymore. It is the reevaluation of these long-held convictions that test the ideas of **exclusivity** and **inclusiveness.**

Designers, as well as a diverse society, must ask, "Whose ergonomics? Whose aesthetics? Whose society?"

Figure 2.7 **Hunter Douglas Teddy Bear Break-Thru Safety Tassel.** (*See Figure 3.78*) (*© 1995, Hunter Douglas, Inc.*)

These are fundamental questions. As the diversity of viewpoints and goals are heard, designers must rise to the occasion and, together, create a new vision of the future.

The Americans with Disabilities Act (the ADA) has focused attention on one of the new principles of design. The first principle is **accessibility,** a concept that stresses ability not **dis**ability—access for all! What impact will this concept/idea/ideal have on the workplace? As a society we can no longer relegate the wheelchair user, crippled, legless, mute, or deaf to the back of the room. They are us and we are them! We **must,** by law, accommodate everyone and we **will** accommodate everyone, and we will be better for it.

The law will impose the second new principle of design, **responsibility,** on the design community. Clean air acts, landfill acts, resource depletion, sick-building syndromes, material reuse, material disposal, natural light requirements, the rain forests, etc., will force designers to act in a more responsible way. It is the responsibility of everyone to ensure that our plant is safe, secure, and fundamentally sound as we pass it on to our children. Without a change in habits, both economic, social, and environmental, we will have beautiful buildings, beautiful interiors, and beautiful chairs with no one to inhabit, work in, or sit on them!

The third new principle of design, **communication,** seems self-evident and obvious—at first thought. But it is a fundamental design principle we violate every day by assuming "they" know what to do, what to say, and how to do it. Designers are assuming too much! We must all be teachers and educators. If designers are not, they are not fulfilling one of the obligations designers must accept. Specifically, to tell clients how, why, what, when, and where their decisions affect how we live, breathe, and navigate our built environment and what effects these decisions have on society in general.

We must make a more pragmatic use of all our senses in constructing the environment, to guide, instruct, and facilitate our use of our built environment. We should permit social responsibility to guide our ecological senses when making decisions about our environment. Letting the concept of **communication** be our guide to interaction and education, there is a chance of the "new design agenda" to make our lives, healthier, happier, and definitely more rewarding.

This agenda will affect our design lives in a major way. Buildings, interiors, products, and services in our built environment will change for the better. Accessibility, responsibility, and communication are not just design education ideas but the **new design agenda.**

Checklist

Stop signs are unambiguous, clear, and universal in their message. Trying to stop a meeting about

Figure 2.8 **Stop Sign.**

"Socially Responsible Design" after being shown a poster that was announcing a series of seminars on the topic "What Is Socially Responsible Design?" was one time I wished for a large portable stop sign. What was being presented was illegible and unreadable. I asked if the idea was **communication.** The reply was that the metaphors and word play [were] what was important. The visual tricks and cleverness with typefaces were the ideas that mattered. The ability to read the information was secondary! The viewer had to be "caught," attention grabbed. I asked, "Whose attention? For what purpose?" The **mess** was the **message.** Deconstructed graphics is a clever way to get attention but the message can be lost or irretrievable. Students need to be educated in Universal Design ideas so that everyone can read, see, listen to, and enjoy their design ideas. The Stop sign is both the media and the message. Its shape and color both signals and alerts.

Bruce Hannah

Hoping to at least get part of the message, the following is a proposal of a list of questions designers should ask of themselves and other designers.

Questions to Designers

Following is a list of questions designers should ask themselves when creating a product.

Why design something that can't be used?
Why say something that can't be heard?
Why write something that can't be understood?
Why draw something that can't be seen?
Why build something that is inaccessible?
Why construct something that can't be climbed?
Why paint something that is invisible?
Why sculpt something that can't be felt?
Why bridge something that can't be crossed?
Who are designers designing for?
What are designers designing?
Where are designers designing?
When are designers designing?
How are designers designing?
Are designers making life elegant for everyone?
How do the blind turn off the lights?
Whose standards are standard?
Whose norms are normal?
Whose solution is universal?
Whose microcosm is worldly?

Designers Should Ask . . .

Who is the design for?
What is the design problem?
Where will the design be used?
When will the design be used?
How will the design be used?

Universal Design is Possible if the Answers to the above questions are . . .

Everyone!
Universality!
Everywhere!
Always!
Universally!

CHAPTER 3

THE HOME AND LIVING—BUILDING COMMUNITY THROUGH ACCESSIBILITY

Designing for the Life of a Family

Creating an environment that will accommodate the transitions as a family grows and ages is the definition of the universal home. Most young couples are able and fit, climbing stairs and accommodating obstacles with ease. As they create a family and age, however, the home environment can become dangerous and inhospitable, by limiting access and endangering children and elderly visitors. Designing spaces, defining products, and accessing services that accommodate the ever-changing mix of a household should be the goal when a new home is created. Having access to their own utensils, playthings, and clothes encourages independence in every member of the household. Likewise, for reasons of safety or age appropriateness, certain places, products, and services need to be protected and off limits. Designing from the beginning with this concept in mind will challenge existing ideals, ideas, and conventions.

Figure 3.1 (*Courtesy of Kim Beasley.*)

Making any space, product, or service in a house fully accessible to everyone may be impossible, but permitting interdependence may be just as important as promoting independence. The young child that can help her grandfather prepare dinner learns more than the child who is excluded because of an inability to reach the kitchen counter or other work space. The near-blind father who can read to his children because there is adequate light fulfills a social contract that reinforces the parent-child bond.

Planning for the eventuality of aging from the designer's first stroke of the computer keyboard will pay off in an easier, more-productive, safer lifestyle. From the simple act of turning on a light to the complex task of bathing, everything we come in contact within the home should be designed for use by a young child of eight to a grandmother of 80.

The simplest changes in the design of tools can change a routine chore into delight. By enlarging the handles of common kitchen tools, OXO made a significant contribution to the ease and safety of everyday tasks. The soft handles cushion the finger grips, making cutting, peeling, paring, chopping, and slicing significantly easier.

Feature: OXO Utensils

Good Grips kitchen utensils designed by Smart Design were influenced by Patty Moore, an expert on aging and universal accessible design. Davin Stowell and Patty Moore shared space together and Patty Moore's influence rubbed off. Davin Stowell was the lead designer on the "Good Grips" project.

Moore wrote a book, *DISGUISED: A True Story*, which described her experience as she traveled throughout the

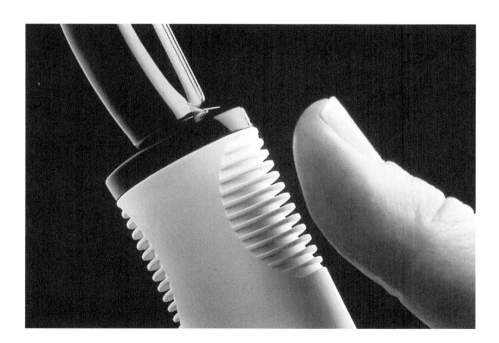

Figure 3.2 **OXO Utensils.** (*Courtesy of Smart Design.*)

United States and Canada disguised as a woman of more than 80 years of age. Her experiences and knowledge helped sensitize other designers to the problems of older consumers and users of kitchen utensils. The cushioned handle and the thumb depression used to establish cutting direction is still finding a huge audience of satisfied consumers. By addressing the conditions of arthritis in the hands and loss of visual acuity, the designers produced a product that not only satisfied the aging community but almost everyone else—a universal design.

"We were trying to make something that everyone would use but also would end up in MOMA, because good design shouldn't be considered special."

Tucker Viemiester of Smart Design
on the "Good Grips" project.

Space: Home Scenario

Designed in collaboration with the Center for Accessible Housing to accommodate everyone as they age or become

Figure 3.3 **Excel Homes.** (*See Figure 3.4*)

disabled. Under the direction of Ron Mace the Center for Accessible Housing has been one of the leaders in accessible design. Coining the term "Universal Design," Ron Mace intended just that—design that was universal in scope and intent. The excel system consists of some 23 plans of standard mass marketable house plans. A variety of accessible and adaptable kitchen and bathroom plans each reflect different standard user needs. They include a collection of designed and specified optional features such as power windows and adjustable counter tops. Through a dealer, the buyer can pick almost any plan with any kitchen and bath, and choose to add whatever additional options best fit his or her needs. The units are factory built with options installed and shipped to the desired location. Since options are catalog standard assembly line choices, the time and cost are lower. (*Courtesy of Center for Universal Design.*)

Space: Home Scenario— Cutaway View of 3-Bedroom Unit

The Excel Homes were designed to meet the changing needs and circumstances of family members throughout their lifetime. The homes are modular in construction and features. Conceptually the buyer can go to a dealer/builder and specify what features and benefits are desired to be built into the house, from the general to the specialized. The buyer orders the house and it is constructed and delivered to the buyer's site.

Mace's goal was to design not only an accessible home but an affordable and approachable one as well. By designing for flexibility and reconfiguration from the beginning Mace was able to create a wide variety of combinations that all provide open plans, wide doors, and accessibility. From the beginning safety was a consideration in the specification of flooring (nonslip, nonglare vinyl or low-pile carpet) to locating railings, switches, and controls at an easy-to-reach height. Every possible detail of everyday life—from the planning level, to covered entrances without steps, to a

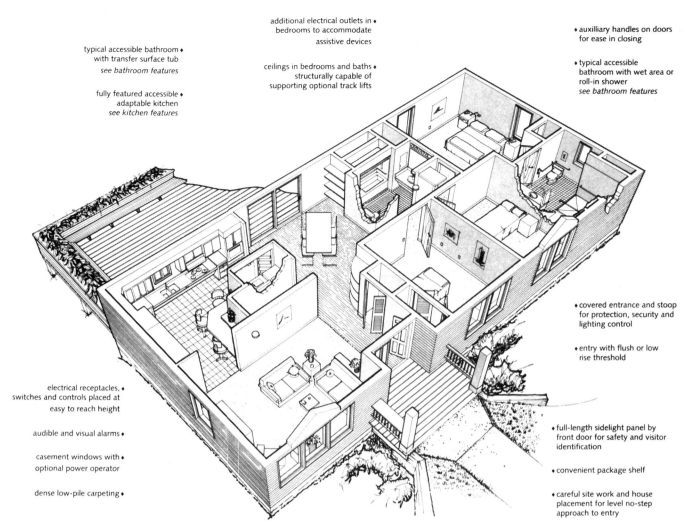

typical accessible bathroom •
with transfer surface tub
see bathroom features

fully featured accessible •
adaptable kitchen
see kitchen features

additional electrical outlets in •
bedrooms to accommodate
assistive devices

ceilings in bedrooms and baths •
structurally capable of
supporting optional track lifts

• auxilliary handles on doors
for ease in closing

• typical accessible
bathroom with wet area or
roll-in shower
see bathroom features

• covered entrance and stoop
for protection, security and
lighting control

• entry with flush or low
rise threshold

electrical receptacles, •
switches and controls placed at
easy to reach height

audible and visual alarms •

casement windows with •
optional power operator

dense low-pile carpeting •

• full-length sidelight panel by
front door for safety and visitor
identification

• convenient package shelf

• careful site work and house
placement for level no-step
approach to entry

Figure 3.4 Accessible Homes Designed by Ron Mace and the Center for Universal Design at North Carolina State University for Excel Homes.

front door with a sidelight so that the residents can identify who's at the door to a shelf next to the front entrance so packages can be set down while the door is opened—was thought out and implemented. *(Courtesy of Center for Universal Design.)*

Space: Home Scenario—Kitchen

The kitchen can be reconfigured and refitted depending on the family's needs. The counters are adjustable from 30 to 36 inches in height.

Not only is the kitchen adaptable after installation, but because it is designed like a car with options, it can be specified to fit the buyers needs from a catalog of standard options. Ron Mace wanted everyone to have the capability of building a unit as basic or as complex as they needed or wanted. *(Courtesy of Center For Universal Design.)*

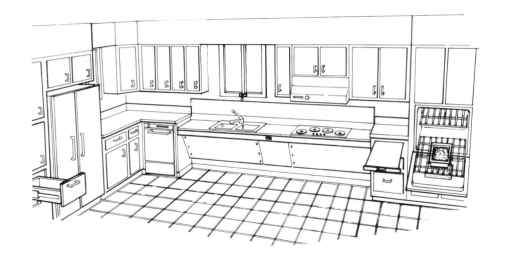

Figure 3.5 **Accessible Homes Designed by Ron Mace and the Center for Universal Design at North Carolina State University for Excel Homes.**

Space: Home Scenario—Bathroom

The bathroom floor plans allow for a variety of planning options, from a roll-in shower to a transfer tub, all with accessibility as the overriding concern. Walls are reinforced

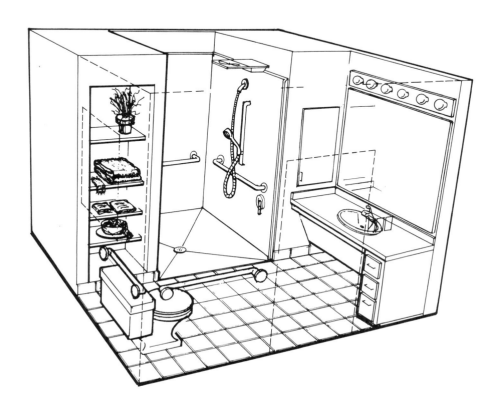

Figure 3.6 **Accessible Homes Designed by Ron Mace and the Center for Universal Design at North Carolina State University for Excel Homes.**

Universal design is a concept or philosophy for design that recognizes, respects, values, and attempts to accommodate the broadest possible spectrum of human ability in the design of all products and environments. It requires sensitivity to and knowledge about people of all ages and abilities. Sometimes referred to as lifespan design or transgenerational design, it encompasses and goes beyond the accessible, adaptable, and barrier free design concepts of the past. It largely eliminates the need for stigmatizing, embarrassing different looking, and usually more expensive, special features and spaces for special people. Universal design is as much a marketing idea as a design concept since products and spaces that are more universally usable are marketable to nearly everyone as well. When well implemented Universal Design can be invisible, marketable, profitable, safe, and both physically and emotionally accessible to most users. In simple terms Universal Design is user-based "good design" carried somewhat beyond the commonly accepted averages in human factors.

Ronald L. Mace FAIA
Program Director
Center for Universal Design
School of Design
North Carolina State University

for grab bars and cabinets can be altered to provide knee space. (*Courtesy of Center for Universal Design.*)

Designing ways for people to live independently, safely, and comfortably is the goal of these homes. As families age, become more complex, and both work and play in their homes, more will turn to the ideas and concepts embodied in these homes.

Figure 3.7 **Barrier-Free Home by Architect Jane Langmuir.**

Space: Home Scenario

Designed as a barrier-free home, intending to be a seamless solution for many of the issues surrounding accessibility and Universal Design. "Why not consider designing for your lifetime, not just your prime time?" Langmuir suggests. Planning can make the transitions in aging enjoyable not dangerous or frightening.

Teaching a course at Rhode Island School of Design and writing a book called *The American Kitchen Revisited,* Jane Langmuir asks questions and postulates solutions to problems of living. Langmuir suggests that open shelving, lower work surfaces, wider doors, and walk-in showers can make our lives easier and safer. This house, designed with the vigorous architectural integrity of a Yankee Cape Cod dwelling and the new spirit of Universal Design, proves that designers can succeed in creating accessible homes for everyone. (*Courtesy of David Lund.*)

Space: Home Scenario

The lowered, open shelves provide not only easy access but also enable a quick, easy inventory of food products. This kitchen offers four different work surfaces; counters, utility cart, table, and island. (*Courtesy of David Lund.*)

Figure 3.8 **Cabinets Barrier-Free Home by Architect Jane Langmuir.**

RANDOM THOUGHTS ON UNIVERSAL DESIGN

"Universal Design is—

1. Design that enhances the dignity and independence of the greatest number of users.
2. Design that can adapt to user-specific needs without compromising the integrity of the product.
3. Design that is aesthetically pleasing.
4. Design that performs to the optimum need.
5. Design that is consumer informed.
6. Design that is sustainable."

Jane Langmuir

Figure 3.9 **Worksurface Barrier-Free Home by Architect Jane Langmuir.**

Space: Home Scenario

The deeper (by four inches) cabinets provide an unobstructed 18-inch-deep work surface, making it easier to slide pots and pans along the surface. (*Courtesy of David Lund.*)

Space: Home Scenario

Pull-out rolling storage utility cart with its 29-inch height eliminates the stooping and reaching associated with un-

Figure 3.10 **Pull-Out Storage Barrier-Free Home by Architect Jane Langmuir.**

dercabinet storage and also provides another work area. (*Courtesy of David Lund.*)

Space: Home Scenario

A high gooseneck faucet with lever handles reduces reaching and, combined with the twin sink, creates a user-friendly work area. (*Courtesy of David Lund.*)

Space: Home Scenario

If this appears to be a traditional, family-oriented room, then Jane Langmuir feels she has succeeded in combining the virtues of Universal Design and accessibility with traditional architectural conceptions. (*Courtesy of David Lund.*)

Figure 3.11 **Sink Area Barrier-Free Home by Architect Jane Langmuir.**

Figure 3.12 **Living Area Barrier-Free Home by Architect Jane Langmuir.**

Figure 3.13 **Shower Barrier-Free Home by Architect Jane Langmuir.**

Space: Home Scenario

The roll-in–roll-out shower is in keeping with the spirit of the house, both architecturally and aesthetically. The simple chair provides seating, but is also a reminder of the elegance and seamlessness of the house. (*Courtesy of David Lund.*)

Space: Home Scenario

Architect Kim Beasley integrated this lift next to the stairs into the front entrance of an existing house, demonstrating that design integrity can be maintained when making homes accessible. (*Courtesy of Kim Beasley.*)

Figure 3.14 **House Lift.**

Kitchen Scenario: Appliances

Choosing accessible appliances and appropriate materials is then followed by sketching a plan that combines them into a working environment. This sketch points out design features that help create an accessible kitchen. The designers planned how they would work in the space and then designed for efficiency and adaptability. This kitchen plan in-

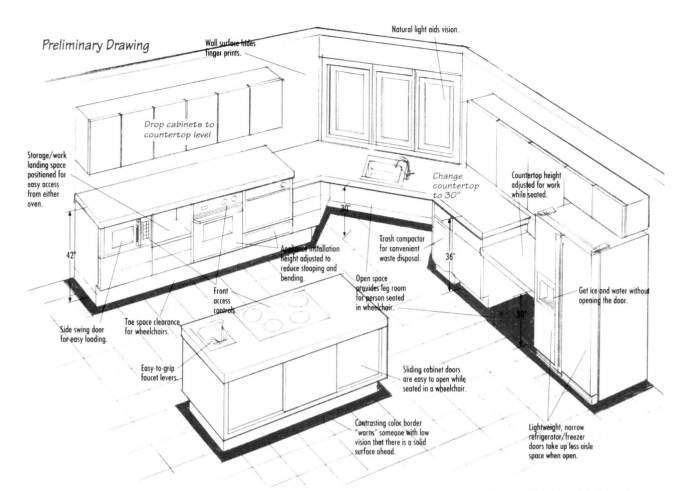

Preliminary Drawing

Wall surface hides finger prints.

Natural light aids vision.

Drop cabinets to countertop level

Storage/work landing space positioned for easy access from either oven.

Change countertop to 30"

Countertop height adjusted for work while seated.

42"

30"

Appliance installation height adjusted to reduce stooping and bending.

Trash compactor for convenient waste disposal.

36"

Front access controls

Open space provides leg room for person seated in wheelchair.

30"

Get ice and water without opening the door.

Side swing door for easy loading.

Toe space clearance for wheelchairs.

Easy-to-grip faucet levers.

Sliding cabinet doors are easy to open while seated in a wheelchair.

Contrasting color border "warns" someone with low vision that there is a solid surface ahead.

Lightweight, narrow refrigerator/freezer doors take up less aisle space when open.

Figure 3.15 **Whirlpool Kitchen: Preliminary Drawing.**

cludes an island that provides a focal point and an approachable work area. The sliding doors provide access without creating obstructions when opened. The second sink lets someone else work independently.

The raised dishwasher and stove reduce stooping and bending. Locating the microwave in the cabinet frees up counter space. Dropping the cabinets to counter level increases accessibility. Various-height counter surfaces (30," 36," and 42") also permit individuals of varying heights and abilities to cook and create in this kitchen. (*Courtesy of Whirlpool.*)

Kitchen Scenario: Appliances

An example of a well-thought-out kitchen designed to accommodate that universal paradigm of grandmother and granddaughter.

Figure 3.16 **Whirlpool Kitchen.**

By positioning the appliances at an appropriate level for the individual performing the task, they become more accessible and reduce stooping and bending. Appliances with front-access controls permit everyone to use them more easily. Adjustable countertop height allows work while seated. A fixed countertop height of 30 inches accommodates both children and adults while seated or standing. Open space under the counter allows someone to sit at the counter and work. A contrasting edge on the countertop signals the transition from countertop to side. Lowering cabinets brings most of the storage into easy reach. The island provides access from all sides and encourages interaction. The contrasting border defines the transition from floor to cabinet, benefiting someone with low vision. Sliding cabinet doors are easier to open and do not obstruct the passageways.

Natural light aids vision and is supplemented with adjustable lighting over the work surfaces. Light switches and outlets are in a contrasting color to the surrounding wall, making them easier to see and use. By using high contrast between counter, utensils (black utensils on a white surface, for example), and tools common tasks become easier and less stressful. Pouring hot coffee into a black cup may be easy for a young or fully sighted person, but to an elderly or visually impaired person it can be difficult—and dangerous. (*Courtesy of Whirlpool.*)

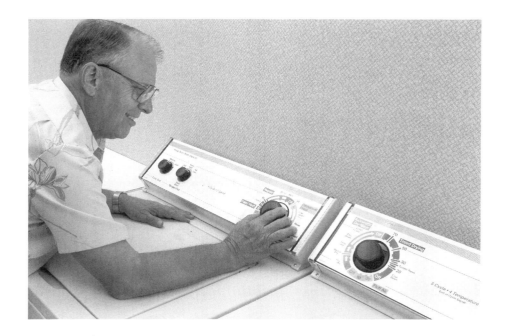

Figure 3.17 **Whirlpool Washer and Dryer.**

Kitchen Washing Appliances

Enlarged typeface on the washer and dryer control panels make operation safer and easier for everyone. Is there some reason why there are two different control panels? If the clear typeface and clear graphics work for low vision they certainly will work for everyone. (*Courtesy of Whirlpool.*)

RANDOM THOUGHTS ON UNIVERSAL DESIGN

Getting to the door is one thing, opening it is quite another. The doorway that is open somehow symbolizes Universal Design, the entrance is permitting entry. Locked doors are barriers to many things but permitting entry maybe only an unkept promise if the door's handle prevents entry.

Bruce Hannah

Product: Handles

Molded of Ultramid nylon, the Hewi door handles are comfortable to the touch and require little maintenance. The

Figure 3.18 **Hewi Inc. Passage Door Lever Handle. Designed by Heinrich Wilke, Rudolph Wilke, and Winfried Scholl.**

nonporous surface is easily wiped clean, is not receptive to bacteria or microorganisms, and maintains a mild temperature despite temperature fluctuations. (*Courtesy of Hewi.*)

Product: Handles

Providing a number of ways to activate a door handle was the solution Lutz Savant sought with his design. The handle announces its location and tapering the keyhole helps locate the lock. The door can be opened by either turning the lever or pushing on the circular lever end. (*Courtesy of Lutz Savant, Pratt Institute.*)

Figure 3.19 **Door Handle. Designed by Lutz Savant, a graduate student at Pratt Institute.**

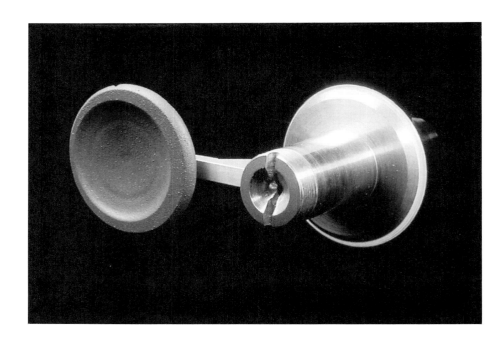

Product: Handles

A small collection of handles inspired by habits and humor that is blind to age, culture, and gender. The coat hanger lever handle holds a coat securely, the hook handle holds a trash bag, the bottle opener handle is useful for torquing a top off a bottle, and the "Pull the Tea Towel" handle makes the towel accessible and pulling the towel extends the handle. (*Courtesy of Six L.T. Wu, Design Age/Royal College of Art U.K.*)

Figure 3.20 **"A Small Collection Of Handles."** Designed by Six L.T. Wu at the Royal College of Art in London for *Design Age* Competition sponsored by the Royal Society for the Advancement of the Arts (RSA). (**Photo: Ivan Coleman**)

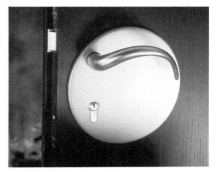

Figure 3.21 **Franz Schneider Brakel (FSB). Designed by Philippe Stark.**

Product: Handles

The PS1's circular backplate boldly confirms the placement of the door handle and the echoing form of the handle indicates the direction the handle should be moved to open the door—downward. (*Courtesy of The Ironmonger, Inc.*)

"How many versions of the ubiquitious "safety" lever are there, each as boring as the next?—Ironmonger is well in front of the pack with distinctly not-boring variations to show that original design will always lead."

John Hurst, for The Ironmonger

Figure 3.22 **Franz Schneider Brakel (FSB). Designed by Johannes Potente.**

Product: Handles

Designed in 1953, this classic door handle, dubbed the "Handflatter," remains a benchmark in expressing the four principles of grip formulated by Otl Aicher in his book *Greifen und Griffe* published by Walther König. Thumb and forefinger are guided automatically. The ball of the hand finds support, and the hand itself finds the correct handling volume. (*Courtesy of The Ironmonger, Inc.*)

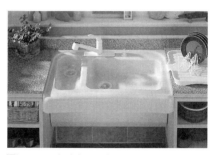

Figure 3.23 **Kohler Assure Kitchen Sink (shown here with Coralais integral faucet).**

Kitchen Fixtures

The faucet, with pull-out spray head, brings the spout to the seated user by taking into consideration not only the obvious considerations for accessibility, such as shallow basins and offset drains, but the limitations of upper-body mobility, reach, gripping strength, and accessibility to work surfaces and appliance controls, Kohler has taken accessibility a step farther. This highly functional sink has a front ledge that gently curves away from the user, bringing the basin closer to a seated user and provides a good handhold. A polystyrene shroud fits under the sink to protect the user's knees from the heat of the pipes. (*Courtesy of Kohler Co.*)

Figure 3.24 **Formica Edges.**

Kitchen Fixtures

Contrasting edges fabricated in Formica Corporation's Surell solid surfacing material not only create an exciting interplay of color but help define the boundary of the work counter. (*Courtesy of Formica Corporation.*)

Kitchen Fixtures

The beveled edge with contrasting colors alerts and warns at the counter edge. (*Courtesy of WilsonArt.*)

Figure 3.25 **WilsonArt Custom Edges.**

Figure 3.26 **Kohler's Finesse faucets shown here with High Country spout.**

Kitchen Fixtures

These faucets and the spout are easy for persons with limited hand or arm movement to use. (*Courtesy of Kohler Co.*)

Kitchen Fixtures

The faucets are activated by a sensor which emits an infrared beam of light for hands-free operation. (*Courtesy of Kohler Co.*)

Figure 3.27 **Kohler's Touchless faucets.**

Kitchen Fixtures

The Heritage Gooseneck, with widespread faucet and wrist blade handles, is a simple and elegant Universal solution to a faucet that can be used anywhere in the home. (*Courtesy of American Standard.*)

Figure 3.28 **American Standard Faucets.**

Kitchen Fixtures

Ceramix Kitchen Combi. Temperature-controlled single-lever combination sprayhead–faucet is a simple and elegant Universal solution to a faucet that can be used anywhere in the home. (*Courtesy of American Standard.*)

Figure 3.29 **American Standard Faucets.**

Kitchen Utensils

The Peppergun grinds fresh peppercorns when you squeeze its handles. Grind size is adjusted by a thumb screw and a loading window on the side allows for easy filling. The one-handed-leveraged operation illustrates how Universal Design can extend a product's use.

Figure 3.30 **Unicorn Peppergun by Tom David Inc. Designed by Tom David.**

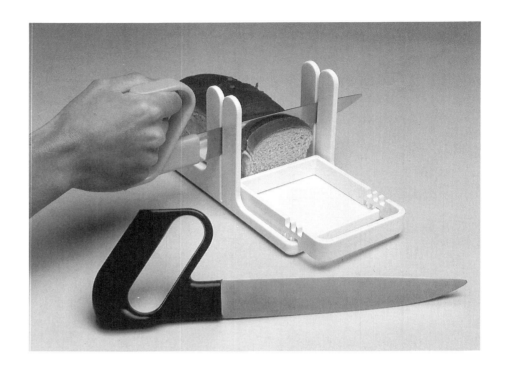

Figure 3.31 **Slicing Aid by ETAC Designs for Independence.**

Figure 3.32 **Cheese Slicer by ETAC Designs for Independence.**

Figure 3.33 **The Chopper and Bowl. Designed by David Stowell and Annie Breckenfield for Smart Design.**

Kitchen Utensils

The design was developed to reduce the stress on the user's hand and wrist when cutting. It uses the strength of both the hand and arm to facilitate cutting. (*Courtesy of ETAC, USA.*)

Kitchen Utensils

The design uses the strength of both the hand and arm to facilitate cutting, which reduces stress on the hand and wrist. (*Courtesy of ETAC, USA.*)

Kitchen Utensils

The handles are larger, making gripping easier, and the blade is contoured to the bowl's diameter. The user needs less pressure and the product is comfortable and safe to use. (*Courtesy of Smart Design.*)

Kitchen Small Appliances

One of the first kitchen products designed that placed a switch into the product so that anyone could turn it on

Figure 3.34 **Cuisinart Food Processor.**

easily and off safely. Designer Marc Harrison worked with the elderly and the arthritic as he developed this universal-use machine that has permeated our lives. (*Design: Marc Harrison, IDSA Professor, Rhode Island School of Design, Providence, RI*)

RANDOM THOUGHTS ON UNIVERSAL DESIGN

"Universal Design is good design because it is design for the user and not design for the designer."

Marc Harrison

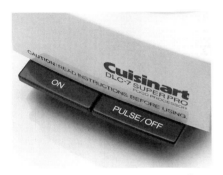

Figure 3.35 **Cuisinart Food Processor.**

Kitchen Small Appliances

The Cuisinart Food Processor lever-action buttons are a good example of high-contrast, simple, clear, and instructive graphics on controls. This is an excellent example of how Universal Design can be so easily incorporated into everyday designs which benefits all of us, not just an isolated group. (*Design: Marc Harrison, IDSA Professor, Rhode Island School of Design, Providence, RI*)

Kitchen Small Appliances

This enhanced jar opener takes away the muscle strain of opening a jar by hand. The switch activates the motor and turns off the top. The jar is pushed up into the cone. This is the original concept for cone-shaped jar and bottle created by an Illinois farmer for his arthritic wife. He built a large unit with welded frame and huge motor. Appliance Science purchased patent rights and developed a small low-cost unit and gear train/cone design. The cone has "rat-tak" type edges that grab the edges of jars, bottle caps, etc. There are two versions: battery-powered and electric. (*Design: Marc Harrison, IDS Professor, Rhode Island School of Design, Providence, RI*)

Figure 3.36 **Open Up Jar and Bottle Opener by Appliance Science. Designed by Marc Harrison.**

Dinnerware

The designer conducted trials testing different-shaped handles to find out which was the most comfortable for older

Figure 3.37 **Tea for Three. Designed by Kit Morris at the Royal College of Art in London for** *Design Age* **Competition sponsored by the Royal Society for the Advancement of the Arts (RSA). (***Photo: Ivan Coleman***)**

and younger users. The form was designed to encompass a large group of users both young and old. *(Courtesy of Kit Morris, Design Age/Royal College of Art, U.K.)*

Dinnerware

The designer was aiming at people over 60 years of age, believing that if older customers could use the product, then younger ones could, also. Redesigning the container for ease of opening and handling eliminates the need for adaptive gadgets that aid opening. The jars are conical in shape with a square lid and easy-to-read labeling. *(Courtesy of Kit Morris, Design Age/Royal College of Art, U.K.)*

Dinnerware

The designer wanted to provide optimum ergonomic convenience while adhering to conventional manufacturing standards. She developed tableware of high design while meeting the correct ergonomics. The teacup can be picked up in a variety of ways—through the hole in the handle, around the top which has a molded-in ridge, or by squeezing the handle—all without appearing to stigmatize. *(Courtesy of Vicki Evans, Design Age/Royal College of Art, U.K.)*

Figure 3.38 **A Jar We Can Open. Designed by Gavin Pryke at the Royal College of Art in London for** *Design Age* **Competition sponsored by the Royal Society for the Advancement of the Arts (RSA).** (*Photo: Ivan Coleman*)

Figure 3.39 **Bonjourno Inclusive Design Tableware. Designed by Vicki Evans at the Royal College of Art in London for** *Design Age* **Competition sponsored by the Royal Society for the Advancement of the Arts (RSA).**

Figure 3.40 **Enable Containers—Easy-Open Containers. Designed by Esther Perera-Borobio at the Royal College of Art in London for *Design Age* Competition sponsored by the Royal Society for the Advancement of the Arts (RSA).**

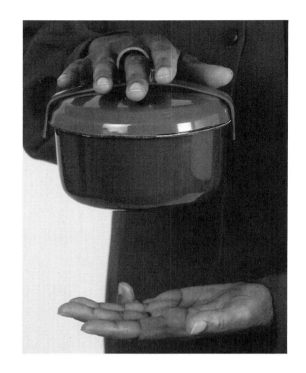

Figure 3.41 **M Cutlery by ETAC Designs for Independence.**

Figure 3.42 **RA Cutlery by ETAC Designs for Independence.**

Dinnerware

The designer wanted to provide food-storage containers, suitable for freezing and microwaving, which are especially easy to hold for people with limited strength and finger control. (*Courtesy of Esther Perera-Borobio, RSA Student Design Awards.*)

Dinnerware

The large, soft handled design accommodates people who have severe arthritic conditions but, to illustrate (and emphasize) the universality of Universal Design, is suitable for everyone else. (*Courtesy of ETAC, USA.*)

Dinnerware

By increasing the diameter and softness of the handles, the design accommodates people who have severe arthritic conditions but is suitable for everyone else. This shows how well function can be combined with form. (*Courtesy of ETAC, USA.*)

Dinnerware

The goblet accommodates most people even those with diminished strength and mobility in their arms. The beaker glass is also appropriate for those with reduced touch sensitivity and coordination. The plate has a raised edge and antislip rubber on the underside. While designed specifically for people with severe arthritic conditions, these are products which make everyday life easier for all. (*Courtesy of ETAC, USA.*)

Figure 3.43 **Goblet, Beaker, and Plate by ETAC Designs for Independence.**

Dinnerware

As the illustration demonstrates, design for accommodation (function) can be as romantic and sensuous as anything that is designed just for form. (*Courtesy of ETAC, USA.*)

Figure 3.44 **Goblet, Beaker, and Plate by ETAC Designs for Independence.**

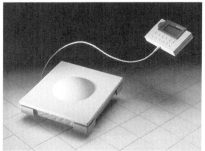

Figure 3.45 **Tanita Smart Scale. Designed by ZIBA Design. (*Photo: Michael Jones*)**

Bathroom

The Smart Scale brings the information to the user by a use of a small control panel that can be mounted within easy reach and sight.

CONTRAST: While it may sound trivial to recommend that black coffee be poured into white cups, it isn't a minor problem to many of the aging and sight impaired, more than 12 million Americans with significant vision loss, that cannot be substantially corrected, are not **legally** blind. As we age we lose large percentages of our eye's capability to receive light; up to 30% less light falls on the retina by age 50. This significant loss creates immediate problems in visual acuity that cannot be corrected by the use of glasses or other prosthetics. A simple graphic might suffice to **clarify** this phenomenon:

1. Black counter, black cup, black coffee, and burnt toast—The perfect designer solution of black on black makes it very difficult to decern and define objects.

2. Black counter, white mug, black coffee, and medium toast—Creates high contrast although the black counter absorbs too much light and therefore decreases available refraction and reflection.

3. White counter, black mug, skim milk, and medium toast—creates high contrast.

4. White counter, white mug, light coffee, and white bread. Graphics two and three demonstrate an appropriate use of contrast, while the first and last graphics, without contrast, become increasingly difficult to see.

The Authors

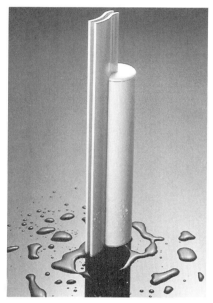

Figure 3.46 **Cleret. Designed by ZIBA Design.** (*Photo: Michael Jones*)

Bathroom

The Cleret epitomizes good Universal Design with a handle big enough and comfortable enough to use. The fact that the form screams "use me—handle me" should be a great lesson in itself.

Bathroom

Demonstrating an easily accessible roll-in–roll-out Freewill shower, a clear, unobstructed wall-mounted Chablis sink

Figure 3.47 **Shower Kohler Bathroom Environment.**

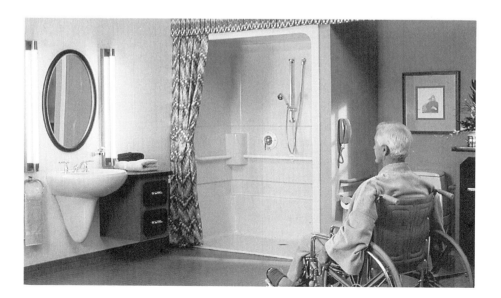

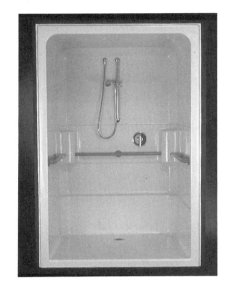

Figure 3.48 **Kohler Freewill Shower.**

Figure 3.49 **Kohler Wall-Mounted Chablis Lavatory.**

with hanging vanity, and the Wellesley water-guard two-piece toilet. (*Courtesy of Kohler Co.*)

Bathroom

An easily accessible roll-in–roll-out shower. (*Courtesy of Kohler Co.*)

Bathroom

The lavatory can be mounted at various heights, providing easy accessibility, and the shroud conceals the piping. (*Courtesy of Kohler Co.*)

Figure 3.50 **Kohler Wellesley Toilet.**

Bathroom

The wall-mounted toilet can be mounted at various heights, providing ease of accessibility. (*Courtesy of Kohler Co.*)

Figure 3.51 **Kohler Bathroom Environment.**

Bathroom

Demonstrating an easily accessible sink and toilet with built-in hand rails and Precedence whirlpool bath. The Precedence is equipped with a watertight door that eliminates the need to step over the rim of the bath. Designed to meet the needs of people with minor chronic conditions that prevent them from lowering themselves into a conventional tub. Putting a door in a tub wasn't easy but it makes the activity of bathing enjoyable and accessible. The bathroom also features the Invitation countertop lavatory and the Highline Lite toilet. (*Courtesy of Kohler.*)

Bathroom

The Precedence model front door provides easy access. (*Courtesy of Kohler Co.*)

Figure 3.52 **Kohler Bath/Whirlpool.**

Figure 3.53 **Kohler Invitation Bath Lavatory.**

Bathroom

The drain is located to the right rear, which positions the drainpipe for easier access. The front rim hangs over the front edge of the countertop, bringing the basin closer to the user. (*Courtesy of Kohler Co.*)

Bathroom

This toilet responds to two design issues: one, accessibility, because of its height, and two, because of its low-water consumption (1.6 gallons per flush), the environment and water conservation. (*Courtesy of Kohler Co.*)

Figure 3.54 **Kohler Highline Lite.**

Bathroom

By squaring off the front the sink is moved toward the front edge of the cabinet, thus making it more accessible. (*Courtesy of Kohler Co.*)

Figure 3.55 **Kohler Bath Lavatory.**

Figure 3.56 **WilsonArt ADA Vanity Bowl.**

Bathroom

Designed to allow easy access when integrated into a bath. The molded one-piece backsplash, bowl, and deck, along with the shallow basin, make this a clean, easy installation. (*Courtesy of WilsonArt.*)

Bathroom

This system of bathroom fixtures and accessories works for all users in a household. The Multi-Track system permits the Pressalit products to move up and down and right and left, providing flexibility in placement, which in turn helps create a safer, more accessible bathroom. The rail mount-

Figure 3.57 **American Standard Preslite Bathroom.**

ing of support arms, lavatory, and shower seating provides adjustment that accommodates a wide range of people and needs. (*Courtesy of American Standard, Inc.*)

Bathroom

The Multi-System and Tilche lavatory adjusts vertically to accommodate everyone from adult to child. It slides easily from left to right to provide extra space between lavatory and toilet if necessary. (*Courtesy of American Standard, Inc.*)

Figure 3.58 American Standard Preslite Lavatory.

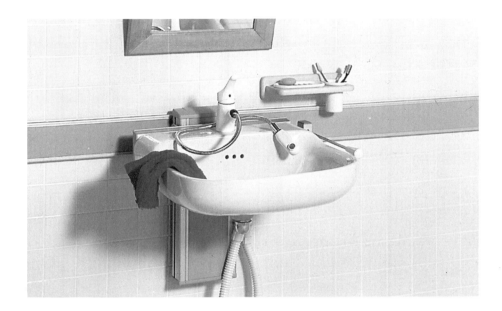

Bathroom

The MultiSystem shower can be fitted with a simple shower chair or a larger contoured chair. Seating and support arms

Figure 3.59 American Standard Preslite Shower.

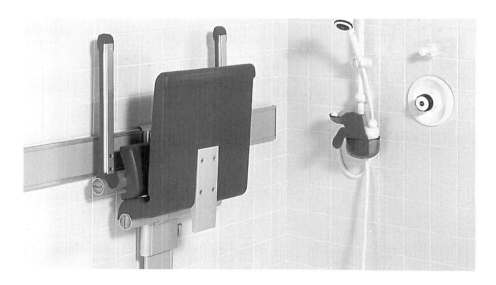

can be easily repositioned both vertically and horizontally. (*Courtesy of American Standard, Inc.*)

Bathroom

The Multi-System toilet, in conjunction with Multi-System support arms, can be easily repositioned both vertically and horizontally to make it highly accessible. (*Courtesy of American Standard, Inc.*)

Figure 3.60 **American Standard Cadet Toilet with Preslite accessories.**

Bathroom

Ceratop is an ADA-approved lever handle that allows infinite one-handed adjustment. (*Courtesy of American Standard, Inc.*)

Bathroom

Anyone who has been surprised by a dose of either too-hot or too-cold water will appreciate Ceratherm. Based on technology from the auto industry, Ceratherm automatically maintains the preselected temperature even if there is a change in supply temperature. An added safety feature limits the temperature of the water to 100 degrees Fahrenheit. Shown with Amarilis Shower system. (*Courtesy of American Standard, Inc.*)

Figure 3.61 **American Standard Faucets.**

Figure 3.62 **American Standard Ceratherm.**

Figure 3.63 **Handheld Shower by Lumex. Designed by Tanaka Kapec Design Group.** (***Photo: Kenro Izu***)

Bathroom

This showerhead functions much like a garden sprayer: the water flows when the handle is squeezed and stops when the lever is released. The handle does not require grip strength or fine hand coordination to hold or activate. Safe, convenient, and easy to use, it also can be operated by foot pressure. Jeffrey Kapek says, "Tanaka Kapek has an ongoing commitment to normalize health care products."

RANDOM THOUGHTS ON UNIVERSAL DESIGN

"I pass through this door. Why can't my friend pass, too? I took my shower. Why can't my grandmother, too? I read the lunch menu. Why can't you?"

Ayse Birsel

Bathroom

Developed as a replacement seat for existing installed toilets the Zoë combines a bidet, toilet, and air freshner all in one. Now everyone can have the convenience of a bidet without the added clutter of an additional product and the safety of remaining in one place for all toiletry functions. The added benefit of remote controls makes this product extremely accessible. (*Courtesy of Zoë Washlet, Toto Ltd.*)

Bathroom

The remote control, which regulates the flow of water and the pressure, features raised buttons with easily distinguished shapes and colors. A seal juggling balls visually demonstrates the rate of flow by how many balls are in the air at once. (*Courtesy of Ayse Birsel and Toto Design.*)

Figure 3.64 **Toto Zoë Combination Toilet and bidet designed by Ayse Birsel.**

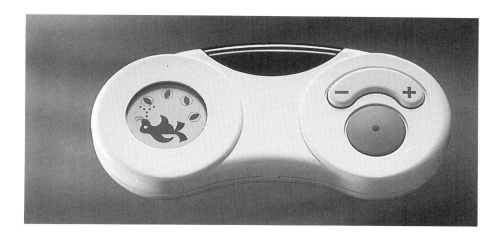

Figure 3.65 **Toto Zoë Combination Toilet and bidet remote designed by Ayse Birsel.**

RANDOM THOUGHTS ON UNIVERSAL DESIGN

"An object or space thoughtfully conceived to serve, support, and stimulate the sensibilities and needs of the disabled and the aging will, by virtue of meeting their extensive requirements, serve all components of society."

Leslie Armstrong

Bathroom

In creating an accessible setting for the "Zoë" toilet, Leslie Armstrong reflected on the "found time" we all use in the

Figure 3.66 **Toto Zoë Combination Toilet and bidet "Zoë" Environment designed by Architect Leslie Armstrong of HLW International LLP.**

Figure 3.67 **Hewi Tub Seat Grab Bar designed by Heinrich Wilke, Rudolph Wilke, and Winfried Scholl.**

toilet. The glass lavatory counter is dropped so the lavatory is accessible while sitting on "Zoë": cabinets on either side are intended to house toilet tissue, reading materials, and a blanket or lap cover for use on the toilet, for bathrooms which are cold and drafty. There's a pull-out, hinged footrest in the bottom of the cabinet directly opposite. (*Courtesy of Leslie Armstrong HLW International and Toto Ltd.*)

Bathroom

Adding a little color to the product sure goes a long way to making it friendly. A bright red grab bar seems to both alert and entice. (*Courtesy of Hewi.*)

Bathroom

Tilting the mirror seems such an obvious a solution and adding the fold-up supports makes using the sink much easier. (*Courtesy of Hewi.*)

Figure 3.68 **Hewi Tilted Mirror and Fold-Up Support designed by Heinrich Wilke, Rudolph Wilke, and Winfried Scholl.**

Bathroom

These products aid people with limited reach due to arthritis and other conditions. They hold a comb, hairbrush, washcloth, bath brush, or a nail file. (*Courtesy of ETAC, USA.*)

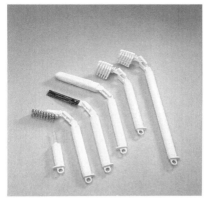

Figure 3.69 **ETAC USA Designs for Independence. "Handy" Extenders designed by A&E Design.**

Home Office

A home workstation designed by William Stumpf & Associates as part of Herman Miller Metaform's Research into the home. It features a reclining chair, a vertically adjustable table, and an accessible compartment work storage area. (*Courtesy of Herman Miller.*)

Figure 3.70 **Sarah.**

Home Office

The desk provides a convenient, large (but not unwieldy) work surface to fit on a person's lap, no matter where the person wishes to work. It accommodates books, paperwork and/or a laptop computer. (*Courtesy of Levenger Tools for Serious Readers.*)

Figure 3.71 **Lap Desk— Levenger.**

Home Office

This circular top desk permits the user to move a computer or papers closer. The top is mounted on a sliding track, allowing the top to be adjusted in or out. The footrest also provides storage space. (*Courtesy of Levenger Tools for Serious Readers.*)

Figure 3.72 **Eclipse Desk— Levenger.**

Figure 3.73 **Island Desk— Levenger.**

Home Office

The desk easily accommodates wheelchairs. It also has a space underneath to store a laptop desk. (*Courtesy of Levenger Tools for Serious Readers.*)

Figure 3.74 **Reader's Table— Levenger.**

Home Office

The height and angle both adjust to allow the person to read in the most comfortable position. Its mobility enables the user to use the desk while in bed or a chair. (*Courtesy of Levenger Tools for Serious Readers.*)

Home Office

Tilted work surfaces are less fatiguing to work at because they put work at the proper angle and don't require the user to lean down and hunch over. An upper shelf holds papers and (open) books at a comfortable angle and reach. (*Courtesy of Levenger Tools for Serious Readers.*)

Figure 3.75 **Editor's Desk—Levenger.**

Home Office

The unique shape and size of this pen allows for a bent thumb, thus eliminating pressure on the thumb and forefinger. People with arthritis in their hands have difficulty in holding most thin-stemmed pens. (*Courtesy of ETAC, USA.*)

Figure 3.76 **Contour Pen—ETAC USA Designs for Independence.**

Home Office

A patented grip filled with Plasmium, a nontoxic gel, has the unique property of "morphing" to the person's fingers. This provides a cushioning effect that softens the grip and eases the tension of writing while also possessing a "memory" so that it returns to a neutral form ready for the next user. This pen epitomizes the term **ergonomic.** Its weight, size, and ease of use make writing available to a very wide audience. (*Courtesy of Willat Writing Instruments.*)

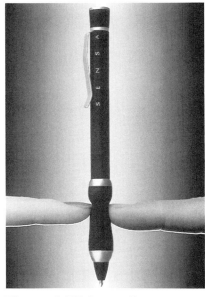

Figure 3.77 **Sensa Pen—Willat Writing Instruments. Designed by Boyd Willat.**

Concept: Safety

Safety and Universal Design go hand in hand. In some ways safety embodies universality because of the unusually high constraints and design criteria associated with safety. The product must be clear and precise in its ease of understanding by the user and must operate almost automatically, since emergencies rarely permit a user time to stop and think or read instructions.

The Break-Thru Safety Tassel works to avoid disastrous results simply by falling apart. No one needs to act, the product does everything. It was developed after a 14-month-old visiting the designers' home was playing near a window and became entangled in the cords. Fortunately

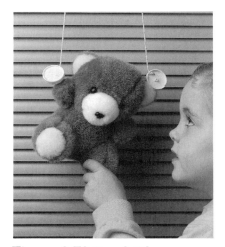

Figure 3.78 **Break-Thru Safety Tassel—Hunter Douglas.**

the child survived, but the designers felt compelled to help prevent similar accidents in the future. The result was the Break-Thru Safety Tassel for miniblinds. By combining the concern for safety with ease of operation a unique product was developed using the elements of Universal Design. (©1995, Hunter Douglas, Inc.)

Home Entertainment

A remote control is a device that, while it makes life a little easier for everyone, is especially beneficial to a person in a wheelchair or otherwise restricted. This epitomizes Universal Design.

Remote technology is relatively old. It began with the sound version of the remote control that operated on "clicks" made mechanically, and the radio-signal-controlled garage door that flew up when someone nearby in the neighborhood changed channels. (*Courtesy of Tandy Corporation.*)

Figure 3.79 **Big-Button Remote Control by Tandy.**

Home Entertainment

Big buttons that light up, along with easily seen and understood graphics and numbers are features every remote control should have. The shape of these remotes offers an easy grip and the base stands the control up so it is always accessible. The shape also helps organize the layout of the buttons. The lower portion, which is smaller and near the grip of the hand, contains the large-scale, frequently used volume and channel up/down buttons, while the flared top incorporates the less frequently used numeric keypad. In addition, the volume control button is **concave** and the channel selector is **convex** allowing easy recognition by touch alone for visually impaired people, or anyone in a darkened room.

A remote control that incorporates a back-lit keypad along with buttons that give tactile feedback begins to approach a universal design. (*Courtesy of Sony Corporation of America.*)

Figure 3.80 **Universal Remote Commanders. Designed by Sony Corporation of America, Design Center.**

Home Entertainment

The **My First Sony** line of products demonstrates the intuitive design principles of everyday life through the use of scale, color, and texture on the product's body and con-

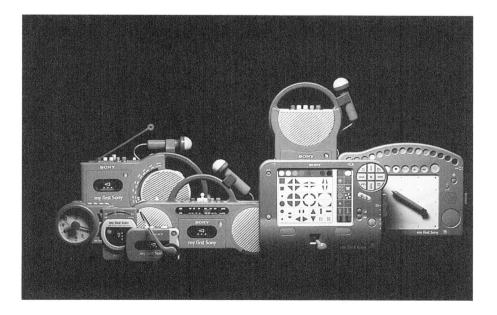

Figure 3.81 **My First Sony. Designed by Sony Corporation of America, Design Center.**

trols. The increasing size of the voice icon control buttons is a tactile as well as visual expression of loudness to indicate volume. The use of the icon also transcends language boundaries as well. With color-coordinated buttons for function distinction, the products use the classic "toy" colors of red, yellow, and blue to clearly demonstrate the functions and the toys remain free of gender color prejudices. The speakers are yellow as are the microphone making the connection both visual and visceral. The handles in the line are all blue while the bodies are red. (*Courtesy of Sony Corporation of America.*)

Product: Thermostat

Using every design technique and all the senses to increase use ability, the Honeywell design team succeeded in creating a universally accessible thermostat. It features large, raised numbers at 50°, 60°, 70°, and 80°F, an enlarged temperature scale (also available in high-contrast black-on-white lettering), and a large ribbed dial that is easy to grasp, specially designed for people with limited strength and dexterity, and allows users to brush or roll the dial. The temperature arrow is oversized, making it easier to read. When the user sets the temperature, the dial makes audible clicks every two degrees. There are also indents which can be felt every two degrees as well. The instructions are in

Figure 3.82 **Honeywell Easy-to-See, Easy-to Use Thermostats: James A. Odom Jr., Senior Principal Industrial Designer.**

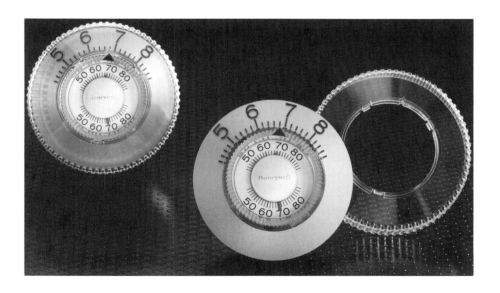

large print or braile. These features all contribute to a truly universal design. The only things missing are voice activation and a speaking mode. (*Courtesy of Honeywell Industrial Design Dept.*)

RANDOM THOUGHTS ON UNIVERSAL DESIGN

"[It is] an approach to creating design solutions that attempt to satisfy user needs across the spectra of age, physical agility, and sensory acuity."

James A. Odom

Indoor Tools

The VersaPak XR cordless electric drill is an example of accessible, responsible design. Cordless products such as electric razors, or electric tools make our lives not only easier but safer, with no power cords to trip over or dunk in water. The VersaPak takes all of this one step further by helping create a responsible, environmentally friendly product stressing the battery design, its interchange ability, and ease of replacement. Careful developmental attention was given to the refinement of the pistol grip and trigger switch to improve comfort and control of the drill. Cordless technology frees the user from the cord restraint. (*Courtesy of Black & Decker.*)

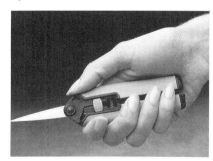

Figure 3.83 **Black & Decker VersaPak 3/8″ Drill. Designed by Robert I. Somers.**

Indoor Tools

The oversized handles are covered in a layer of thermoplastic rubber that absorbs the shocks experienced when cutting fabric. Springing the scissor blades to open after each cut reduces the pressure on the hands and joints and helps increase the efficiency of cutting. (A screw easily adjusts the tension on the spring to suit the user.) A slide lock located on

Figure 3.84 **Fiskars Softouch Scissors designed by the Fiskars Design Group in a response to the needs of an aging population.**

the upper handle close to the thumb safely locks the blades in a closed position. The American Society on Aging cited the Softouch scissors for design excellence by meeting the needs of an aging population and contributing to functioning independence and self-esteem. (*Courtesy of Fiskars, Inc.*)

Figure 3.85 **Vantage.**

Outdoor Tools

The Vantage line is a range of mechanical garden tools designed by Seymour Powell to provide more power for less effort. The main item is a pair of garden secateurs (pruning shears) which offer mechanical advantage and can be extended for greater reach even to a full tree-height pruning cutter. Equipped with controls that increase the mechanical advantage two to three times through the use of hydraulics, the Vantage tree trimmer is transgenerational in its design and function. (*Courtesy of Seymour Powell.*)

Outdoor Tools

The Woodzig utilizes scaled-down chainsaw technology to empower users with good cutting ability with little effort.

Figure 3.86 **Woodzig Power Pruners by Blount, Oregon Cutting Systems Division. Designed by ZIBA Design.** (*Photo: Michael Jones*)

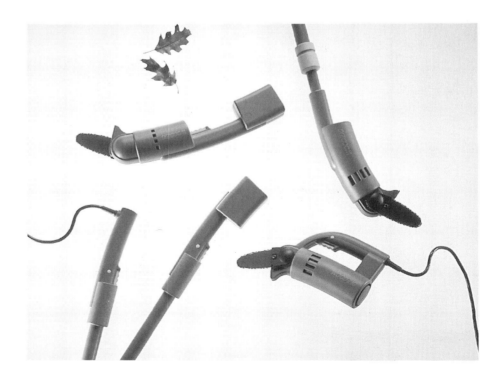

Communication

Picking up the phone and asking to speak to someone by simply saying, "Can I speak to Grandma?" has a familiar ring to it. Many can remember doing just that when as small child, the only difference is that today it is a machine which recognizes my voice and not an operator. Voice-recognition dialing allows a caller to connect with friends or the family doctor or emergency numbers with a simple word. This aids a person with reduced vision and/or someone who needs to make an emergency call and, due the nature of an emergency, has no time or presence of mind to consult a directory. (*Courtesy of Smart Design.*)

Figure 3.87 **Voice Dialing.**

Personal Hygiene

A collaboration between the furniture manufacturer Herman Miller and the consulting firm Design Continuum resulted in a prototype personal hygiene system that met a series of design principles. The design principles established a set of ground rules for design and development of new products and services and are worth reiterating.

1. **Design should be bias-free.** Not require youth or complete ability; it helps a broad range of people of different ages.

2. **Design should be well mannered.** It should take into account the way people will live or work and how this changes with age.

3. **Design should be substantial.** It should evince a physical presence—renewable, durable, not temporary; it ages gracefully as people age.

4. **Design should be congruent.** It should demonstrate the principles behind the design.

5. **Design should be provocative.** It should enable activity and discourage passivity by offering people the chance to do things for themselves.

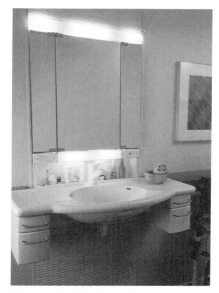

Figure 3.88 **MetaForm Personal Hygiene System. Herman Miller/Design Continuum/Gianfranco Zaccai IDSA.**

6. **Design should be comforting.** It should expand and strengthen ability and resolve and emphasizes prevention.

7. **Design should be playful.** It should allow for delight, surprise, and play.

The MetaForm concept fulfills the design principles of Universal Design, inviting participation and encouraging thoughtfulness. It is a prototypical statement of design meeting the challenge of universality by inviting participation in a daily ritual.

Gianfranco Zaccai and Design Continuum began work on the System in 1988, when David Levy of Herman Miller Research called to discuss a project that would enable disabled and elderly individuals to live more independently. Mr. Zaccai was particularly interested in the project because his elderly parents were entering a time of life when caring for themselves at home was becoming increasingly difficult. Mr. Zaccai attributes much of his insight into the problems of aging to his concerns for his parents' well-being. Focusing on personal hygiene, Design Continuum began their research and development by creating guidelines that would be implemented during development of the system. (*Courtesy of MetaForm.*)

Design Guidelines

· Develop an in-depth understanding of the specific needs of disabled individuals: physical, psychological, and economic.

· Find where the needs of the potential users, especially the very young and very old, and their caregivers converge.

· At the state, national, and international levels identify current and emerging standards, codes, and legislation that may affect design, installation, and purchasing decisions.

· Identify broad-based convenience, image, and prestige features that can serve to broaden market appeal and further destigmatize the product.

- Identify opportunities to reduce the overall costs of product, installation, and labor.

- Test design concepts with a broad spectrum of potential consumers.

from Innovation *Fall '93*

Each module is described as a node of related activities. Each node is designed to remove barriers and hazards or adjust gracefully to the needs of different users. (*Courtesy of MetaForm.*)

Personal Hygiene

The shower node includes a barrier-free floor drain, support bar, and accessory rail and the water, lighting, ventilation, and communication column. (*Courtesy of Design Continuum.*)

Personal Hygiene

An extension of the shower node, the tub node is a familiar bath which is made of a resilient material, "Pesilent." The

Figure 3.89 **MetaForm Personal Hygiene System— The Shower Node by Herman Miller/Design Continuum.**

Figure 3.90 **MetaForm Personal Hygiene System The Tub Node by Herman Miller/Design Continuum.**

rim of the tub allows for a sitting transfer, and the bow front facilitates a wheelchair transfer and allows greater water volume. As disabilities become more severe a hydraulic transfer chair that operates off normal household water pressure is installed easily to the rail system. (*Courtesy of Design Continuum.*)

Personal Hygiene

The toilet seat is adjustable in height from 10.5 to 24 inches to allow for semisquat elimination and to facilitate transfer. The bowl rotates into a wall cavity, where it is cleaned and sanitized automatically, freeing up floor space and increasing the flexibility of the bathroom. A built-in sprayer–dryer bidet adds to the convenience and safety of the toilet. (*Courtesy of Design Continuum.*)

Personal Hygiene

This personal hygiene station adjusts vertically as a unit (sink, mirror, and storage) from 24 to 42 inches accommodating both seated and standing users.

The adjustability and adaptability demonstrated by the MetaForm Personal Hygiene System set a standard for all manufacturers of toilets, sinks, and baths. Having physical examples of accessibility and adaptability ideals will help

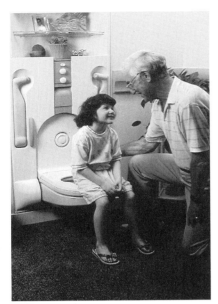

Figure 3.91 **MetaForm Personal Hygiene System— The Toilet Node by Herman Miller/Design Continuum.**

Figure 3.92 **MetaForm Personal Hygiene System— The Sink Node by Herman Miller/Design Continuum.**

understanding just what Universal Design means. (*Courtesy of Design Continuum.*)

RANDOM THOUGHTS ON UNIVERSAL DESIGN

"Both my parents became sources of insight and design ideas for MetaForm and are as responsible for the design of MetaForm as myself or the rest of the group at Design Continuum."

Gianfranco Zaccai

Concept: Prescription Medicine Dispenser

The Pill Safe originated as a project initiated by the Design Business Association (UK) and *Design Age*. The Pill Safe has two components: a portable handset and a base station. The handset is the dispenser and can be programmed to dispense up to 28 dosages. The base station both recharges and programs the handset.

Figure 3.93 **Pill Safe by Indes Design.**

Medication is one of the most rapidly growing areas of health care cost, an area where efficacy of treatment is related to taking medication of the correct types at the right time. In conjunction with Dr. Jonathon Fisk, who provided technical information about drug regimes and consumption of medications, Indes proposed the development of a medication-dispensing device for pills and capsules. The product provides a means to administer medications in a controlled manner while providing the patent with reminders to consume medications, prevents consumption of incorrect medications, and provides health care professionals with consumption data. (*Courtesy of Indes Design Consultants.*)

Figure 3.94 **Pill Safe by Indes Design.**

Concept: Prescription Medicine Dispenser

When the handset alerts the user (by either audio, visual, or vibrations), the green push button, which also flashes, is depressed. This sets the access-time sequence and opens the door. (*Courtesy of Indes Design Consultants.*)

Concept: Prescription Medicine Dispenser

The user slides back the access door to expose the medication compartment, which contains medication to be taken. (*Courtesy of Indes Design Consultants.*)

Figure 3.95 **Pill Safe by Indes Design.**

Concept: Prescription Medicine Dispenser

Medication is accessed tipping out the contents. The access-time sequence will activate the correct time, shut the door,

Figure 3.96 **Pill Safe by Indes Design.**

and then move another compartment into position. (*Courtesy of Indes Design Consultants.*)

Concept: Prescription Medicine Dispenser

When the handset is mounted in the base station, it recharges and can be reprogrammed. (*Courtesy of Indes Design Consultants.*)

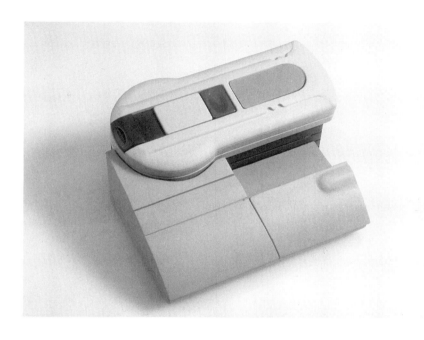

Figure 3.97 **Pill Safe by Indes Design.**

RANDOM THOUGHTS ON UNIVERSAL DESIGN

"Universal Design is good design because it is design for the **user** and not design for the **designer.**"

Robert Anders

Personal Care

Robert Anders, Professor of Art & Design at Pratt Institute, teaches Universal Design with a holistic approach. He challenges students to respond to everyday problems in uniquely beautiful ways. Benson Kravtin's tooth flosser turns on and off simply by squeezing the bulb-shaped han-

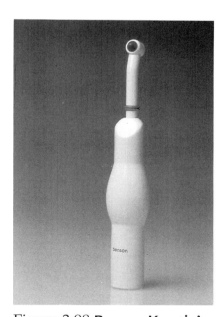

Figure 3.98 **Benson Kravtin's Tooth Flosser designed by Benson Kravtin, a graduate student at Pratt Institute.**

dle. Almost anyone can use this elegantly simple tool with ease, comfort, and safety. (*Courtesy of Benson Kravtin.*)

Figure 3.99 **Portable Hair Dryer. Designed by En-Bair Chang, a graduate student at Pratt Institute.**

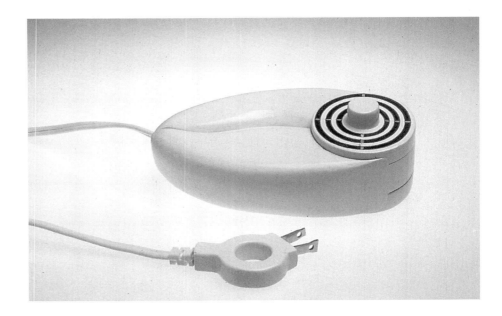

Personal Care

This product features a plug designed for people who have difficulty in grasping (for insertion or removal) standard tapered plugs. En-Bair Chang solved the problem for everyone by simply molding a hole in the plug. Dexterity becomes less of a problem when inserting or removing the plug, simply because there is a variety of ways to hold it—through the hole, grasping the rounded outside edge, or placing the fingers on both sides of the hole. (*Courtesy of En-Bair Chang, Pratt Institute.*)

Peppermill

The turning action was developed to allow one-handed and two-handed operation. The rubber "O" rings on the barrel provide a sure grip. The designer wanted to design and develop a product that was responsive to a wide audience while maintaining a high level on design quality. (*Courtesy of Joe Laybourn, RSA Student Design Awards.*)

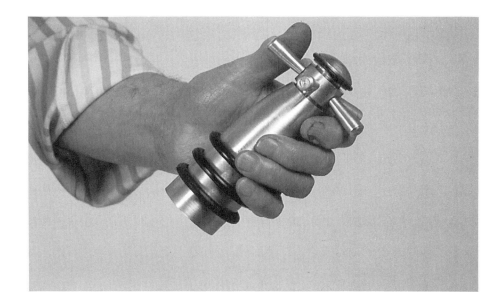

Figure 3.100 **Ease of Use Pepper Mill. Designed by Joe Laybourn at the Royal College of Art in London for** *Design Age* **Competition sponsored by the Royal Society for the Advancement of the Arts (RSA).**

HOME TRANSITIONS TO REMEMBER

Transitions from one space, service, or product to another often present barriers whether physical or psychological.

1. Threshold Access: Home Entrance; Doors

2. Vertical Assent: Stairs; Elevator; Escalator

3. Dining Access: Dinnerware; Chairs; Tables

4. Kitchen Access: Appliances; Counters; Cabinets

5. Living Room Access

6. Bedroom Access

7. Recreation Access

8. Bathroom Access: Appliances; Fixtures

9. Technological Access: Communications; Computers

10. Outdoor Access: Patio, Pool, and Play

CHECK LIST
Accessible Home

1. Use color and texture to alert and instruct.

2. Use high-contrasting materials or colors to delineate changes in counter surface and height. Round the edges of countertops. Avoid needless changes in levels.

3. Lighting should be adjustable in intensity and placement. Natural light is more diffused making areas easier to see. Use motion detectors to turn the lights on and off.

4. Use lever handles on all doors, appliances, and cabinets, as they're easier to open and close.

5. Use uncomplicated, simple faucets with lever (blade) handles and temperature controls.

6. Use ground-fault interrupter switches. Choose cordless when possible.

7. Avoid highly polished floors. They may become slick and dangerous and they also reflect glare, which can distract and/or disconcert people.

8. Do all entrances, doorways, and ramps provide clear, easy access for everyone? Be aware that stairs, entrances, and doorways may present hazards. Are there any clear tripping or slipping hazards? Mark edges of stairs, ramps, platforms, entrances, and exits by changing texture or using a high-contrast color.

9. Can everyone easily use the bath, toilet, and sinks in spite of limitations in mobility and reach. Are water faucets accessible? Do they accommodate people with limited hand or arm strength? Are towels accessible? Are mirrors accessible? Are walls reinforced for grab bars? Do the tub rims allow for a sitting transfer? Is the toilet seat height adjustable? Are appliances, such as hair dryers, accessible and safe? Are users protected from scalding pipes and waters? Do shower and baths accommodate shower or contour chairs? A bathroom/kitchen may have to be rearranged once it is installed.

10. Appliance controls using high-contrast (i.e. dark lettering on a light background) are generally easier to see and operate. Are they clearly marked? Are

there multiple sense indicators? Does an appliance prevent injury by announcing cycles and temperatures?

11. Are controls such as locks, thermostats, light switches, power outlets, and telephone outlets, reachable and accessible to everyone? Is hazardous use preventable? Can small children be protected from danger?

12. Are appliances, utensils, tools, and controls accessible and easily manipulated? Do users have a choice of grips? Are the grips large enough (small enough) for everyone? Do the colors contrast?

13. Do small appliances, such as hairbrushes, scissors, etc. have extended padded handles?

14. Are switches accessible? Highlight the location of switches and receptacles and doors with contrasting paint or wallpaper.

15. Are cabinets accessible? Use D-shaped handles on cabinets. Contrast the handle color and the cabinet. Color-code different cabinets by using different-colored handles. Are the cabinets a comfortable height to prevent stooping? Can the height be adjusted? Are cabinets altered to provide knee space? Are ceiling-mounted cabinets low enough for children and adults? Do open doors, cabinets, or shelves present hazardous conditions? Side-opening doors on cabinets are easier for everyone to use and do not obstruct passageways .

16. Does tableware take into account the ergonomic needs of its users?

17. Does a product prevent unintended actions?

18. Do warning–alerting devices have audio, visual, and vibrating alarms or signals?

19. Are containers and packages easy to open?

20. Do the safety features take into account everyone—no matter what their height, age, or mobility—who will come into contact with them?

CHAPTER 4

THE OFFICE AND WORK

Feature: Herman Miller Aeron Chair

The Aeron Chair is the latest chair design produced by the collaboration of Bill Stumpf and Don Chadwick and the furniture manufacturer Herman Miller. Bill Stumpf and Don Chadwick created a chair that is forgiving and supportive. The name "Aeron" refers to "sitting on air." By stretching a specially designed "Pellicle" mesh over a frame the chair allows air to circulate freely as one sits on it. It provides a comfort level that far surpasses most any other seat material by evenly distributing the body weight on the seat and back. The unique tilt mechanism adjusts automatically to allow people to move easily from forward to reclined positions. Arms, seat height, and back tension can be adjusted, plus, a lumbar support that can be adjusted both in height and depth make this an ultimately adjustable chair. Stumpf and Chadwick designed three sizes of Aeron chairs—small (A), medium (B), and large (C)—all with identical performance capabilities. The chair is adaptable in its design and its use and responsible in its use of materials. (*Courtesy of Herman Miller.*)

Figure 4.1 **Aeron Chair.**

As the office becomes more like the home and vice versa the facilities become more adaptable and friendlier, if

in no other way than visually. The Accessible Office, whether at home or business, works for everyone. The concept of making every entrance way, hall, room, and workstation fully accessible eliminates the need to create "special situations for special people." Everyone benefits from the accessible workplace whether they are disabled or not.

Most offices, until the Americans with Disabilities Act (ADA) passed in January 1990, weren't accessible. The ADA mandates that all commercial and public facilities be barrier free, providing access to people with disabilities. The ADA made many workplaces adjust to suit everyone. Adjustability means adaptability and making the equipment in the office responsive to the individual is the real goal. Ease of adjustability will lead to ease of adaptability. Adjusting the components of an office is easier that adjusting the furniture in an office.

Awareness of this fact and having the solutions available to create barrier-free access to the office for all is the goal of this chapter.

Office Space Scenario

Figure 4.2 **Lighthouse Model.**
(*Photo © Jeff Goldberg,*
ESTO.)

Developing a Design Process that Is Inclusive

The Lighthouse Headquarters in New York City stands as a model of accessibility especially for people with impaired vision as well as everyone else. Mitchell/Giurgola Architects, and their consultants, Whitehouse and Company, Way Finding and Graphic Consultants, and H. M. Brandson and Partners, Lighting Designers and The Lighthouse faced a unique design opportunity. They needed to design a facility that maximized independence and access for people with vision, hearing, and mobility difficulties. A comprehensive process focused on Lighthouse researchers, consumers, and staff to evolve design development guidelines. Designing the navigation Signage system demonstrates a methodology that should be used in every building situation. It was an inclusive process that produced a clear result: A navigation system applicable to any space. The following groups were consulted. (*Courtesy of Mitchell/Giurgola Architects and Whitehouse and Company.*)

CONSULTANT GROUPS:

1. **The Environmental Group**—Researchers and staff concerned with clarity of circulation, and quality of lighting, color, contrast, audible communication, and safety.

2. **Orientation and Mobility Instructors**—concerned with how people move through space, horizontally and vertically.

3. **The Lighthouse Consumer Council**—Deal with orientation, access, and environmental considerations affecting Lighthouse consumers.

4. **User Groups**—to test the effectiveness of Signage mock-ups and tactile maps.

GUIDELINES WERE ESTABLISHED IN THE FOLLOWING AREAS:

1. **Color and Contrast**—Use colors to create borders that define spaces; choose appropriate contrasting colors

as borders, generating acceptable brightness contrasts with little or no glare.

2. **Lighting**—Design lighting that optimizes responses to light for people who are visually impaired as well as those with normal sight. H. M. Brandston and Partners used traditional fixtures, modified to appear lighted at a distance and to produce uniform, nonflashing, soft, diffused light.

3. **Signage**—Design signage to respond to users who also have physical and cognitive impairments making it universal.

4. **Orientation and Mobility**—Arrange floor plan organizations to remain constant from floor to floor with consistent locations for rest rooms, fire stairs, and lobbies. Waiting areas and main circulation areas were kept separate, and curves and nonright angles were avoided because orientation techniques for the blind are based on rectilinear space.

Testing Concepts

Using architectural mock-ups of rails, stairs, floor textures, elevator call buttons, workstations, furniture, tactile maps, sign plaques, audible components, and lighting fixtures the goals were tested and refined.

By using this common-sense approach Universally Accessible Design Solutions permeate the final design.

The Lighthouse is the world's first facility when architects, engineers, and lighting and graphic designers, together, developed a high level of accessibility. The Lighthouse is a benchmark in accessibility and Universal Design. The solutions in place at the Lighthouse provide a unique opportunity to study and understand navigation systems that allow everyone to find their way independently.

Figure 4.3 **Lighthouse—
Typical Floor Plan.**

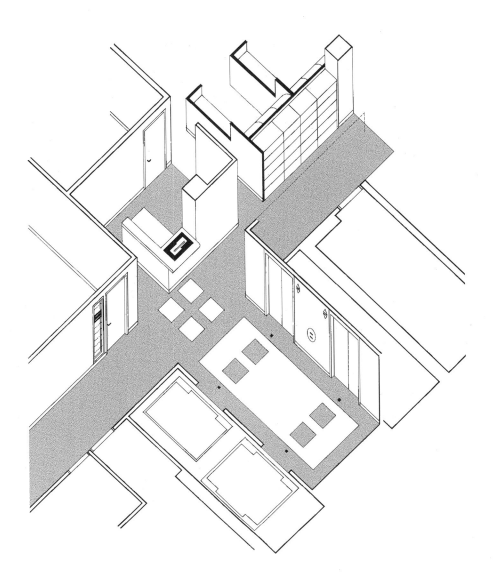

Office Space Scenario

Transitions are defined by contrasting magenta door frames with warm white walls. Dark purple and mauve floor tile patterns indicate transitions from reception areas to elevators to corridors. Visual, tactile, and lighting cues are provided to reinforce and reassure as passage is made about the building. Every design opportunity was taken to make getting around clear precise and **elegant.** Natural light from oversized windows and nonglare light fixtures produce an interior devoid of harsh light level changes. (*Courtesy of Mitchell/Giurgola Architects and Whitehouse and Company.*)

Office Space Scenario

An inclusive Signage system that uses every device available to reach as wide an audience as possible: A high-contrast visual display (white figure on a black ground); a large-scale blue tactile triangle identifies the men's room, a large-scale red tactile circle identifies the women's room; and a 45-degree tactile "ledge" displays Grade 2 braille and a special tactile alphabet. In addition "talking signs" announce conference rooms, rest rooms, and stairways to visitors carrying special handheld receivers. Elevators are also provided with verbal identification of each floor and directs people to a reception area equipped with floor-specific tactile maps. (*Courtesy of Mitchell Giurgola Architects and Whitehouse and Company.*)

Figure 4.4 **Lighthouse—Way Finding and Signage. Designed by Roger Whitehouse.**

💡 RANDOM THOUGHTS ON UNIVERSAL DESIGN

Universal Design is design for everyone. It is user based, and based on all users. It demands that the designer study and understand the full spectrum of perceptual viewpoints and needs of all users. Users are individuals, they are not young or old, sighted or vision impaired, well educated or poorly educated, male or female, black or white, large or small. They are all those things, and every possible shade and nuance in between. Universal Design means not thinking in terms of "them and us" but of understanding that "we are all **us.**" Universal Design does not mean "one size fits all" design, it means that it responds to all. Sometimes redundant responses are appropriate and necessary. Not everyone's needs can be accommodated all of the time, but Universal Design requires that all the available resources are used in the most effective way to make the environment accessible to the greatest number of users at any one time, and no one is given preferential treatment.

Roger Whitehouse

Office Space Scenario

Braille and tactile lettering on the handrail indicate floors. The handrail is painted in sharp contrast to the wall and floor and is continuous, with breaks at exit points. The risers and leading edges of stairs contrast with the color of the tread. (*Courtesy of Mitchell Giurgola Architects and Whitehouse and Company.*)

Figure 4.5 **Lighthouse— Stairwell.**

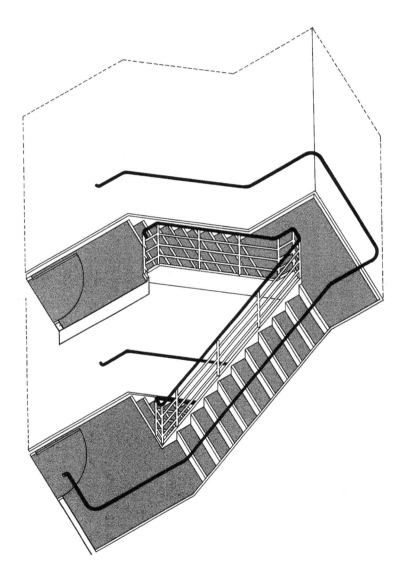

Figure 4.6 **Lighthouse—Main Lobby.**

Office Space Scenario

The information desk in the main entrance serves as an orientation point for those entering and exiting. Tactile strips on the floor indicate stair locations and seating areas, and a trailing rail with tactile marks indicates doors and stairs. (*Courtesy of Mitchell Giurgola Architects and Whitehouse and Company.*)

Figure 4.7 **Lighthouse—Furniture/Workstation/Knoll.** (*Photography Andrew Bordwin.*)

Office Space Scenario

A typical workstation flooded by natural light, easy-access Reuter overhead storage, nonglare highly reflective work surfaces, adjustable chair, and unobstructed single-level work area. This workstation highlights good, straight forward office architecture. (*Courtesy of Lighthouse.*)

Office Space Scenario

This building demonstrates that designers need not abandon traditional symbolism of a raised main entryway because a ramp with compatible symmetry will be integrated

Figure 4.8 **Thomas F. Eagleton Courthouse, St. Louis, MO. Designed by HOK.**

☼ RANDOM THOUGHTS ON UNIVERSAL DESIGN

"And justice for all" may also mean equal access for all or, maybe if you need to go to court, at least you can do it with dignity. Being carried up the grand staircase of a design is not a very fitting way to arrive for a date in court.

Bruce Hannah

into the site design. A solution that includes everyone—from conception—demonstrates that accessibility doesn't necessarily destroy traditional design value systems. (*Courtesy of Hellmuth, Obata, Kassabaum, Inc.*)

Office Space Scenario

Site plan of inclusive entrance. (*Courtesy of Hellmuth, Obata, Kassabaum, Inc.*)

Figure 4.9 **Thomas F. Eagleton Courthouse, St. Louis, MO. Designed by HOK.**

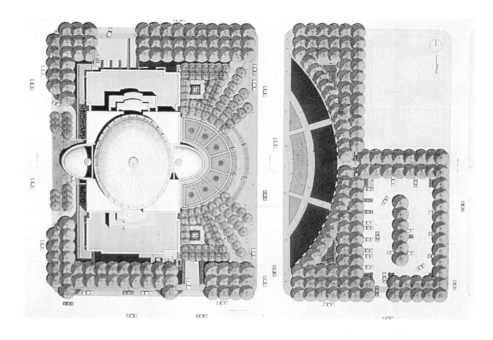

Office Space Scenario

The need to provide an accessible route to the Mississippi River public promenade was a condition of approval by the

Figure 4.10 **Federal Reserve Bank, Minneapolis, MN. Designed by HOK. Currently under construction.**

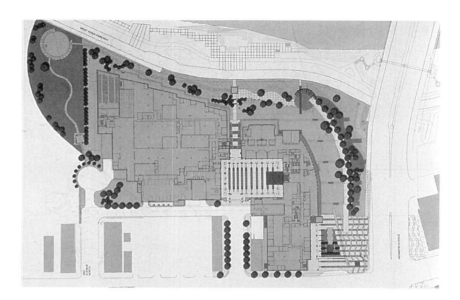

city of Minneapolis. A gradually descending ramp was designed by HOK that met the challenge and, again, accessibility wins out with a beautifully accessible plan. (*Courtesy of Hellmuth, Obata, Kassabaum, Inc.*)

Office Space Scenario

A close-up of the access route. (*Courtesy of Hellmuth, Obata, Kassabaum, Inc.*)

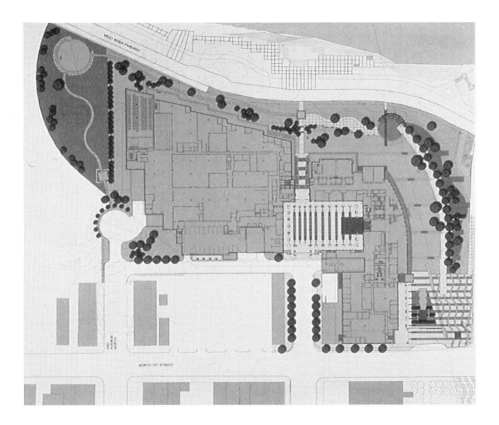

Figure 4.11 **Federal Reserve Bank, Minneapolis, MN. Designed by HOK. Currently under construction.**

Office Space Scenario

Architect Dirk Kramer refinished the green marble floor by honing and sealing, and removing the high gloss and slippery surface to create a surface that met both the design criteria and the access codes. The handrail serves both as a guide and support and provides a discrete barrier from the artwork. The railing also serves as a handrail at a stair accessing a retail space. (*Courtesy of Gwathmey Siegel & Associates Architects.*)

Figure 4.12 **717 Corning Building, Fifth Avenue, New York City. Designed by Gwathmey Siegel & Associates.**

Office Space Scenario

Detail of handrail. (*Courtesy of Gwathmey Siegel & Associates Architects.*)

Figure 4.13 **717 Corning Building, Fifth Avenue, New York City. Designed by Gwathmey Siegel & Associates.**

Figure 4.14 **Knoll Boomerang Tables.**

Office Tables

Designed by John Rizzi as a solution to adjustability in the office. One model features a unique Counterforce system that allows users to reposition table height with a fingertip-control mechanism. The tables are designed to let users sit or stand comfortably while they work. Workers can adjust their keyboard height and tilt. Interaction tables work with other office furnishings to respond to changing needs. They can be used to expand a desk or add a secondary work surface. Biomorphic shapes and soft rounded edges invite reconfiguration and regrouping of surfaces for a variety of uses. (*Courtesy of The Knoll Group.*)

Figure 4.15 **Steelcase Sit-Stand Workstation.**

Office Tables

These units provide complete, dual-surface adjustability in the full range from standing to seated operation. They are fully automated. (*Courtesy of Steelcase*)

Office Tables

Manually adjustable bases that permit adjustment from a sitting position of 26 inches to a standing position of 39 inches. Available as a round, square, or rectangular, or split top on all of Howe's product lines. (*Courtesy of Howe Furniture Corporation.*)

Figure 4.16 **Howe Adjustable-Height Tables.**

Office Tables

Designed by Niels Diffrient, the Tutor furniture system consists of a lightweight modular table and track elements that can be rearranged in a wide variety of configurations to meet the needs of any group learning environment. The Tutor system also accommodates computer and audio-visual technologies with flexible-wire management. (*Courtesy of Howe Furniture Corporation.*)

Figure 4.17 **Howe Tutor Tables.**

Office Tables

Designed by Niels Diffrient, the Tutor furniture system consists of a lightweight modular table and track elements that can be rearranged in a variety of workplaces. Tutor also accommodates wheelchair users. (*Courtesy of Howe Furniture Corporation.*)

Figure 4.18 **Howe Tutor Tables.**

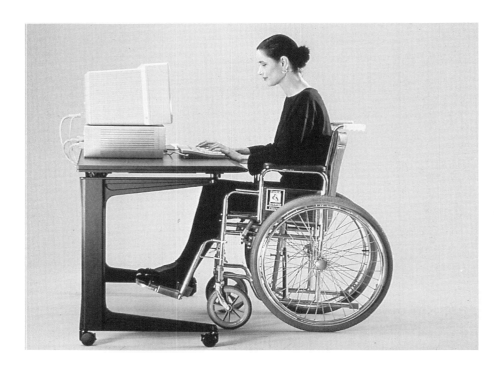

Figure 4.19 **Vecta Ballet K-Base Table.**

Figure 4.20 **Wilkhahn Mobile Desk.**

Office Tables

Douglas Ball on designing the Ballet Table, "My early sketches of the table suggested a dancer in flight." Being able to move furniture when and where you want it is a universal problem. The ballet table solves this problem and the ability to link and add components just makes it that much better. (*Courtesy of Douglas Ball.*)

Office Desks

The mobile desk comes to you. The top tilts for relaxed writing and part of it remains horizontal so that pencils and equipment won't roll off. The height, however, cannot be adjusted. (*Courtesy of Wilkhahn.*)

Office Desks

Mobile servers roll on four casters and have various surfaces and storage bins to accommodate a variety of uses from catering to audio-visual equipment to overhead or slide projectors. It provides a simple solution to accessibility. (*Courtesy of Wilkhahn.*)

Figure 4.21 **Wilkhahn Mobile Servers.**

RANDOM THOUGHTS ON UNIVERSAL DESIGN

UNIVERSAL WORKSTATIONS

Any workstation should be usable by most people. The height and width of a work space should be determined by a worker's ability to both reach and easily see objects placed on a flat surface or shelving placed above the work space at a 45-degree angle. That demands that work spaces be adjustable and easily modified.

Lighting should be mobile and the intensity and direction of the light should be easily controlled to meet the specific needs of the individual. Thirty percent less light falls on the retina at age 50 than at age 30.

Work surfaces should maximize the reach of an individual, determined by the individual's arm span and ability to reach objects from a sitting position. The work surfaces should be adjustable and easily modified.

Services such as telephone, data, and cable should be approachable and accessible.

George Covington

Office Workstations

The goal of the Power-Lift Desk was to provide a product that increases productivity and efficiency and reduces stress and fatigue at work. Touch-sensitive controls position the U-shaped work surface at any height between 23 and 48

Figure 4.22 **Workstations Power-Lift Desk. Designed by Dr. Deborah S. Kearney.**

Figure 4.23 **Workstations AccessiFile. Designed by Dr. Deborah S. Kearney.**

inches or tilt between 0 and 30 degrees. This unparalleled adaptability puts work, computers, and equipment at the worker's beck and call. (*Courtesy of Workstations.*)

Office Workstations

AccessiFile creates a space to work where all the files are available and there is a place to work on them whether you are seated (by folding down a side) or standing (by folding up the top). (*Courtesy of Workstations.*)

RANDOM THOUGHTS ON UNIVERSAL DESIGN

"Universal Design is beyond form and function to include human factor considerations which support the body with adaptable and flexible particulars of grip and reach requirements."

Dr. Deborah S. Kearney

Office Workstations

With carousellike revolving shelves, this file "cabinet" brings the work to you. (*Courtesy of Workstations.*)

Office Workstations

"People are not straight lines, they don't have sharp corners or edges," says Stephen Barlow-Lawson. **"Human beings need to fit with the tools they use rather than fit the tools to their curves."** The Biomorph System presents various configurations for secretarial, managerial, and executive workstations in kidney shapes with soft edge treatments. By adding an independently adjustable keyboard support tray and adjustable platforms to accommodate equipment and acces-

Figure 4.24 **Workstations Roto-File. Designed by Dr. Deborah S. Kearney.**

sories, the Biomorph workstation grows and reacts to the user. (*Courtesy of Biomorph/Stephen Barlow-Lawson, ID Design.*)

Figure 4.25 **The Biomorph Computer Desk. Designed by Stephen Barlow-Lawson.**

RANDOM THOUGHTS ON UNIVERSAL DESIGN

"The issue is not so much—what a great idea! as—how did we all get it so wrong for so long?

"Our work turns out this way because we think about users, not because we're constantly conscious of the Universal Design concept."

Geoff Hollington

Office Workstations

Herman Miller's Relay furniture designed by Geoff Hollington is a group of freestanding desks, tables, credenzas, bookcases, storage units, and movable screens. The desks feature adaptable tops that adjust in height, tilt, and also flip up to provide work surfaces to accommodate most uses. It is particularly well suited to the transitional work space that a lot of us are facing, between home and office. With its wide range of top sizes and base configurations offices can be constructed from a simple desk to a complex of interactive workstations. (*Courtesy of Herman Miller.*)

Figure 4.26 **Herman Miller Relay Furniture. Designed by Geoff Hollington.**

Office Workstations

Screens and work surfaces that move and flex to our work habits, encourage good work habits and different working positions. (*Courtesy of Herman Miller.*)

Figure 4.27 **Herman Miller Relay Furniture. Designed by Geoff Hollington.**

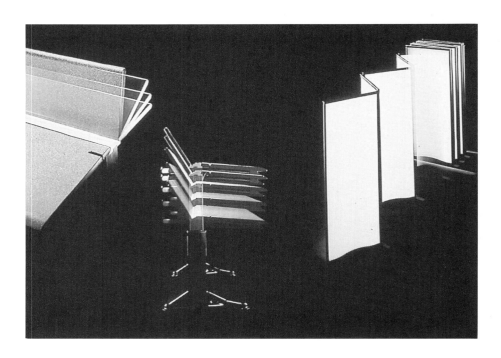

💡 **RANDOM THOUGHTS ON UNIVERSAL DESIGN**

Perhaps it's time that designers forget about designing yet another good-looking thing and accept the much greater responsibility of creating something that benefits society.

Douglas Ball

Figure 4.28 **Herman Miller Relay Furniture. Designed by Geoff Hollington.**

Office Workstations

Work areas evolve as projects change and people move. The Relay line permits workers to easily reconfigure their environment to meet those changes. (*Courtesy of Herman Miller.*)

Office Workstations

Personal activities and workstations can be adjusted easily. Fine-tuning a workstation brings work **to** you rather than you **adjusting to** the work. (*Courtesy of Herman Miller.*)

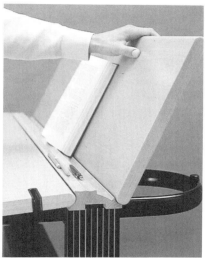

Figure 4.29 **Herman Miller Relay Furniture. Designed by Geoff Hollington.**

Office Workstations

Activity products consist of surface shapes, tools, and accessories that include mobile tables, carts, electronic posts, a bench, screens, and marker walls. Activity tables come in eight different shapes that easily combine into a traditional table or can be grouped into a variety of forms such as a circle, oval, wave pattern, or half moon. The tables can be moved easily by lifting the front edge, as with a wheelbarrow, and pushing or pulling them on their wheeled legs. (*Courtesy of Steelcase.*)

Figure 4.30 **Steelcase Activity Tables. Designed by Douglas Ball.**

Office Workstations

The cart comes in two sizes with three shelves, to provide storage, a work surface, and media support. (*Courtesy of Steelcase.*)

Figure 4.31 **Steelcase Activity Carts. Designed by Douglas Ball.**

Figure 4.32 **Douglas Ball's Race System by Haworth.**

Figure 4.33 **Douglas Ball's Race System by Haworth.**

Office Workstations

Doug Ball designed the Race System to give unprecedented adaptability. Change is the norm in offices as jobs are redefined and reworked. This system's vertical and horizontal adjustability allows everyone to personalize access to their work. (*Courtesy of Douglas Ball.*)

Office Workstations

The cantilevered work surfaces provide unrestricted movement side to side. The continuous upper rail allows the unlimited repositioning of overhead storage. The lower beam supports storage that has unlimited horizontal movement. "There is a sense of turf, a sense of privacy with easy communication, so essential to effective office function," says the designer. (*Courtesy of Douglas Ball.*)

Figure 4.34 **Provox Workstation by Fisher-Rosemount Systems, a division of Emerson Electric. Designed by Fitch Inc. (*Photo: Mario Carrieri*)**

Office Workstations

Integrating the modular furniture support system with the GUI (Graphical User Interface) was a dramatic departure from industry norms. Hardware and software integration was the driving force behind this design. Provox workstations are flexible enough to serve a wide range of industry and user applications and they are ergonomically adjustable for each user. (*Courtesy of Fitch, Inc.*)

Office Workstations

A workstation demonstrating the relationship between the worker and the equipment. Locating all the equipment in horizontal (keyboard, mouse pad, etc.) and vertical planes (multiple screens, copy stand, etc.) clearly establishes a comfortable, easily understood working environment. (*Courtesy of Fitch, Inc.*)

Figure 4.35 **Provox Workstation by Fisher-Rosemount Systems, a division of Emerson Electric. Designed by Fitch Inc. (*Photo: Mario Carrieri*)**

Office Workstations

Components are categorized as perimeters, workplanes, technology support, stowaways, organizers, and power and communications equipment.

The perimeters are delineated by screens that attach to either walls or panels. Workplanes are horizontal work areas. "Stowaways" are storage and filling. Technology supports are carts, bags, and holsters that permit easy mobility.

Figure 4.36 **Haworth Crossings.**

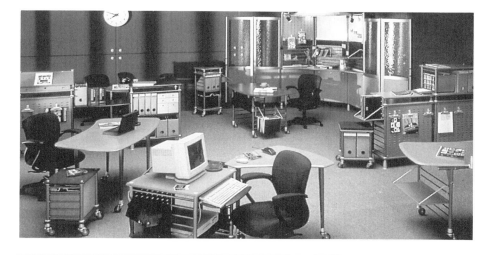

 **RANDOM THOUGHTS ON UNIVERSAL DESIGN**

"Universal Design is the creation and arrangement of objects so that age and physical limitations are not obstacles to their use."

Jeff Reuschel, Manager
Haworth Industrial Design Studio

Organizers provide organization and paper management. Using these components users can construct unique, adaptable, and changeable offices. (*Courtesy of Haworth, Inc.*)

Office Workstations

Crossings is an extension of the worker. Its components change as the situation dictates, allowing work to flow; it reacts to the worker, letting people rearrange furniture to express their needs. (*Courtesy of Haworth, Inc.*)

Concepts

Niels Diffrient has won just about every major design award, is the coauthor of *Humanscale 1/2/3/4/5/6/7/8,* and lectures and teaches design at various schools. The Diffrient system was commissioned by Sunar Hauserman, but unfortunately never made it to production. It stands as a benchmark and still challenges designers with its insight of the fully adaptable office. *(Courtesy of Niels Diffrient.)*

Figure 4.37 **Haworth Crossings.**

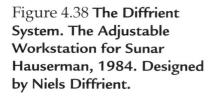

Figure 4.38 **The Diffrient System. The Adjustable Workstation for Sunar Hauserman, 1984. Designed by Niels Diffrient.**

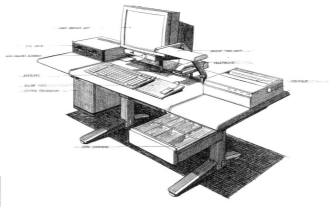

Office Workstations

"Another principle that I came upon early was that if I am designing this for the individual, to match his or her needs, then that implies that each workstation is an isolated island. Everything within that workstation must adjust to his or her scale."

Figure 4.39 **The Diffrient System. The Adjustable Workstation for Sunar Hauserman 1984. Designed by Niels Diffrient.**

Niels Diffrient in Leading Edge, *1984*
(Courtesy of Niels Diffrient.)

Concepts

This was designed as a solution to an office scenario that predicts workers will "camp" when they find themselves in need of a work center. "Camping" is a phrase coined by the Haworth design team that created the Office-in-a-Box" concept. This self-contained office product concept is portable and weighs less than 50 pounds when empty. *(Courtesy of Haworth, Inc.)*

Figure 4.40 **Haworth's Office-in-a-Box developed by the Haworth Industrial Design Studio.**

Office Workstations

The philosophy behind "Office-in-a-Box" is that the worker "owns" the workstation. All work, personal materials, and equipment can be left in the box. The box can be closed up with work in progress and returned to later. All necessary outlets for power, telecommunications, and cabling are located in the lid's hinge area. Ample storage areas and accessories such as a wastebasket, mail slot, tackboard, and even a LAN monitor are built in. Accessible in every way, this box is certainly a step in the right direction. *(Courtesy of Haworth, Inc.)*

RANDOM THOUGHTS ON UNIVERSAL DESIGN

"Universal Access is [the] starting point. Delight without descrimination is the goal."

Robert Edward Reuter

Figure 4.41 **Haworth's Office-in-a-Box developed by the Haworth Industrial Design Studio.**

Office Cabinets

Responding to the problem of opening an overhead door Robert Reuter and a team of Knoll engineers developed the Reuter overhead. A pneumatic-action door allows the user to open and close the cabinet door easily from a standing or seated position, with the touch of a finger. An optional U-shaped door handle makes the Reuter overhead universally accessible. *(Courtesy of The Knoll Group.)*

Figure 4.42 **Reuter Overhead, The Knoll Group.**

Office Cabinets

Meridian's loop-style and curve-style pulls make opening and closing a file draw easier for everyone. Offered in two styles of loop and curve to accommodate every condition in the office. A simple, elegant solution to opening a file drawer. (*Courtesy of Meridian Files.*)

Figure 4.43 **Meridian Files Enhanced Access Pulls.**

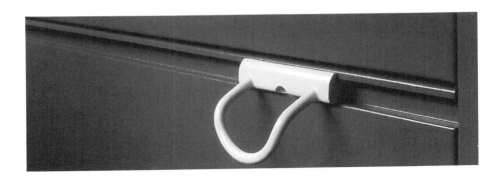

Office Cabinets

The position of locks may seem minor until they can't be reached. Meridian developed a locking system that allows the user to position the lock in any location on stacked lateral files, permitting the user to decide where the lock should be. (*Courtesy of Meridian Files.*)

Figure 4.44 **Meridian Files Lock Location.**

Office Cabinets

A personal mobile pedestal has a file drawer beneath and space for supplies on top. (*Courtesy of Herman Miller.*)

Figure 4.45 **The Puppy Rolling Storage Herman Miller Relay. Designed by Geoff Hollington.**

Office Cabinets

Companion puts storage where you want it. It also features a hinged work surface that lifts up when needed. Companion's hidden top compartment has a hinged lid that also acts as a copy holder. (*Courtesy of The Knoll Group.*)

Figure 4.46 **Rolling Storage. The Knoll Group, Faithful Companion: a personal pedestal. Designed by Jonathan Crinion.**

Office Accessories

The Surf collection of ergonomic accessories was created as a "foot-print form" derived from natural movements. The biomorphic shapes echo the curves and contours of the human body. The Surf collection of accessories includes a wrist rest, mouse pad, footrest, and lumbar support, each designed to help computer users maintain a comfortable, relaxed work position. (*Courtesy of The Knoll Group.*)

Figure 4.47 **Surf by Designers Ross Lovegrove and Stephen Peart for The Knoll Group.**

Office Accessories

A large-button solar calculator with easy-to-read soft, gentle-to-the-touch buttons. (*Courtesy of the Milano Series, International Products Ltd.*)

Figure 4.48 **Moda 1 by Milano Series.**

Figure 4.49 **Adjustable Keyboard Support by Bruce Hannah for The Knoll Group.**

Office Accessories

It allows the user to position the keyboard anywhere to accommodate changing work conditions and habits. (*Courtesy of The Knoll Group.*)

Office Accessories

This line of accessories organizes in a place of the user's choice and by any desired system. An organized workplace is safer, clearer, and much more productive. (*Courtesy of The Knoll Group.*)

Figure 4.50 **Orchestra Accessories. Designed by Bruce Hannah and Ayse Birsel for the Knoll Group.**

Office Chairs

Using "pressure maps," Knoll engineers determined the curvature of the supporting shell and refined the chemistry of the foam padding, creating a chair that rates very high in comfort and long-term support. With adjustable arms, tilt, forward tilt lock, tilt tension, back angle, and back height adjustments, the Parachute chair can be configured to the user's need. (*Courtesy of The Knoll Group.*)

Figure 4.51 **Parachute. Designed by Dragomir Ivicevic for The Knoll Group.**

Office Chairs

"Comfort is often described as 'the absence of stress.' So that, if you are made comfortable, you just take it for granted. That is exactly what I want to happen. I don't want people to notice."

Niels Diffrient in Leading Edge, *1984.*

The adjustable task chair series states the ergonomic chair problem three dimensionally. Adjustable arms, back, and seat height and tilt are all integrated into a cohesive expression, clearly the necessary dimensional requirements. Again, a benchmark for any designer attempting to design an office chair. (*Courtesy of Niels Diffrient.*)

Figure 4.52 **Diffrient Chair System. The Adjustable-Task Chair for Sunar Hauserman, 1984. Designed by Niels Diffrient.**

Office Chairs

This line of chairs features a synchronized tilt mechanism that enables the seat to tilt more slowly than the backrest, to keep feet flat on the floor, thereby reducing stress on the upper legs and lower back. Combined with tilt tension adjustment and pneumatic seat height adjustment, along with forward seat tilt and back height adjustment, this chair accommodates almost everyone in the office no matter what their needs or requirements are, or what task is being performed. (*Courtesy of The Knoll Group.*)

Office Chairs

Modus seating adjusts automatically—when the user leans forward, the seat tilts down, and the farther a user leans back, the resistance increases. Minimalist upholstery consisting of a "breathable" black polamide elastic membrane stretched across the slightly springy backrest supports the back of the user. (*Courtesy of Wilkhahn.*)

Figure 4.54 **Modus by Wilkhahn.**

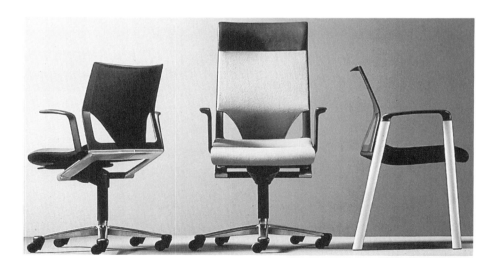

Office Chairs

Rapport is a highly adjustable chair designed to be adjusted as you sit in it. It features a lumbar pillow that moves vertically through a four-inch range to offer lumbar support, arm rests that move in and out as well as up and down independently, the seat moves front to back three inches to accommodate various leg lengths, and a seat that tilts forward for intensive task work, to level, to slightly reclined. All of this can be accomplished with the control located on the arm rest support. (*Courtesy of Steelcase.*)

Figure 4.55 **Rapport by Steelcase. Designed by David Jenkins and David Hodge.**

RANDOM THOUGHTS ON UNIVERSAL DESIGN

"Not only did we want Rapport to be inviting, enclosing, and warmer, but to also include adjustments that are innovative, accessible, and accommodate the needs of today's office workers."

David Hodge
Steelcase

Office Chairs

Criterion's adjustable arms allow fingertip control to adjust arms up and down independently within a four-inch range. Each arm has a four-inch-width adjustment providing eight inches total width adjustment. (*Courtesy of Steelcase.*)

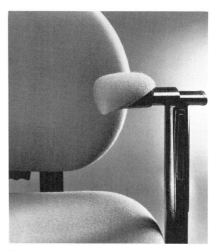

Figure 4.56 **Criterion by Steelcase. Modular Adjustable Arm.**

Office Chairs

Criterion Plus, designed for larger people and people who require more room in a chair, will support up to 500 pounds. Simple-to-use levers adjust seat height, seat and back tilt, back height, and tension. The seat can be mechanically adjusted to three seat depths. (*Courtesy of Steelcase.*)

Figure 4.57 **Criterion Plus by Steelcase.**

 RANDOM THOUGHTS ON UNIVERSAL DESIGN

"Design is most beneficial when it is seen as a creative process that is used by people to improve some aspect of their lives, whether it is to plan a garden, shape a vessel, or compose the elements of a structure in a beautiful way."

David Jenkins
Steelcase

Figure 4.58 **The Prelude Chair by Trendway.**

Office Chairs

A full line of body-friendly chairs. Almost everything can be adjusted, including the back height, seat height and depth, seat and back angles, and, optionally, arm height and the distance between the arms. (*Courtesy of Trendway.*)

Concept: TeamBoard

The TeamBoard supports the teamwork approach by connecting the spontaneously generated idea immediately to the computer screen. It uses pressure-sensitive technology to convert the written images to computer bytes instantly. The mobility of the TeamBoard puts it where everyone can use it, most anywhere. (*Courtesy of Egan Visual.*)

Figure 4.59 **Egan Visual Mobile TeamBoard.**

Concept: Podium

While attending the Roscoe Awards presentation in 1993 Stephen Barlow-Lawson witnessed Dianne Pilgrims' unhappiness with the inaccessibility of the podium. Sensing a design opportunity, Stephen conceived the adjustable Biomorph line of workstations featuring flexible, adjustable work surfaces. The podium features height adjustment from 25 to 45 inches with fingertip control, a "hands-free" script holder which keeps papers in place, and a discrete state-of-the-art microphone which is readily adjustable and shaped to accommodate seated users. (*Courtesy of ID Design.*)

Figure 4.60 **Biomorph Universal Podium. Designed by Stephen Barlow-Lawson.**

Lectern

A lectern designed to meet the needs of all users. This product demonstrates Universal Design beautifully. It dimensionally accepts chairs and provides height adjustment from 34 to 44 inches. It also features a built-in clock, lighting, lockable casters, and microphone mounting clips. *(Courtesy of Egan Visual.)*

Figure 4.61 **Egan Visual Inc. ADA Lectern.**

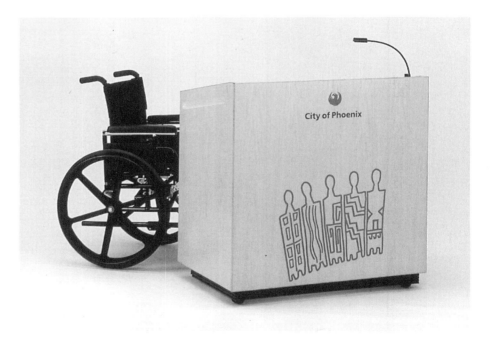

Figure 4.62 **Highlighting Marker by PaperMate/ Gillette Company. Designed by Tanaka Kapec.**

Writing

Writing seems to be fairly straightforward task until it becomes painful. Many people have trouble controlling the tip of a highlighter. This design features a steady, reliable grip, allowing the user to make a steady pass with the pen, thereby improving accuracy and reducing fatigue. (*Courtesy of Tanaka Kapec Design Group.*)

Career Clothes

The collection challenges the way fashion is perceived. The choice of knitwear makes the clothes comfortable and easy to care for and the designer tailored the clothing for ease in dressing. (*Courtesy of Jennifer Lesley Knight,* Design Age, *Royal College of Art U.K.*)

Figure 4.63 **Ageless Fashion. Designed by Jennifer Lesley Knight at the Royal College of Art in London for** *Design Age* **Competition.**

OFFICE TRANSITIONS TO REMEMBER

Transitions from one space, service, or product to another often present barriers whether physical or psychological.

1. Threshold Access: Building Entrance; Office Entrance; Hallways

2. Vertical Assent: Stairs; Elevator; Escalator

3. Reception Access

4. Aisle Access

5. Workstation Access

6. Technological Access: Communications; Computers

7. Meeting Room Access: Doorways; Chairs; Tables

8. Restroom Access: Doorways; Fixtures; Facilities

9. Ancillary Equipment: Copier; Printer; Supplies; Lighting

10. Cafeteria Access: Counters; Chairs; Tables

✓ CHECK LIST
Accessible Office

1. Are entrances, doors, platforms, stairways, ramps, and elevators accessible, are they easy to use, and do they accommodate everyone? Are handrails clearly defined, painted in sharp contrast to the walls, and are continuous with breaks at exit points? Do the risers and stair edges contrast with the color of the tread?

2. Are floors, walls, and shelves clearly delineated? Changes in color and texture provide clues to way finding in buildings. Are the floors nonglare?

3. Are the floors and walls in contrast to the seating and to each other?

4. Are aisles, workstations, toilets, cafeterias, and meeting rooms accessible to everyone? Avoid rough surfaces and protruding or hanging objects in aisles and walkways.

5. Are work surfaces adjustable in height and tilt to meet the needs of everyone? Easily adjustable work surfaces provide variety and ease. Round or oval pedestal tables are approachable by almost everyone, from all directions. Rounded corners on furniture, combined with soft edges, make furniture easier to grip, safer, and are nicer to be around.

6. Work surfaces should be highly reflective but nonglare and neutral in color. Avoid very dark (mahogany) or very light (white) surfaces. Raise and contrast edges on surfaces to delineate and clarify boundaries.

7. Is the keyboard support adjustable? An easily adjustable keyboard support can provide a variety of working positions, from sitting to standing. Use a wrist rest, palm rest, or arm supports if necessary.

8. Is the monitor adjustable? An adjustable monitor support, which can be raised, lowered, and tilted, can easily position the VDT properly. A document support located on the same plane as the VDT can reduce eye strain. Reduce glare on the monitor screen by changing location or adding a polarizing filter.

9. Is the chair adjustable—in overall height, back and seat height, tilt, tilt tension, and arm height. Does it provide lumbar support?

10. Is the lighting adjustable and accessible? Task lighting should be adjustable both in light direction and intensity. Natural light is best.

11. Is Signage clear and intuitive? Use more than one sense for signaling and Signage. Use signs that talk. Use signals that beep, flash, and vibrate. Provide tactile information on walls and floors. Maximize the number of people who can respond to signals. Use high-contrast colors.

12. Are controls accessible? Embossed controls on elevators, chairs, tables, accessories, and work surfaces can give clues to direction and provide a sure grip.

13. Are controls such as switches, alarms, and buttons accessible? Are handles, switches, outlets, receptacles, and thermostats accessible?

14. Are copiers, supply rooms, break areas, and file cabinets accessible to all?

15. File drawer pulls should be looped to provide easy access to everyone. Labeling should be clear and easily read.

16. Are locks accessible? Can they accommodate all users?

17. Are telephones and data communication accessible? Are the power, cable, and data outlets accessible?

18. Are floor plan organizations constant from floor to floor with consistent locations for restrooms, fire exits, and lobbies?

19. Adjustability means adaptability. All equipment, when possible, should adjust—chairs, work surfaces, lighting, and accessories.

CHAPTER 5

THE SCHOOL AND LEARNING

Equal access to education is made easier with the help of modern technology. As the electronic classroom becomes a reality differences in ability will diminish. The dream of individualized instruction is available now. Individual growth and advancement can be greatly assisted by aides and devices, which provide a more level playing field. Invisible sensory impairments can be more easily compensated for with technology.

When I attended grammar school, everything was tied down. The seat was connected to the desk in back, and so on. The simple idea of having free-floating chairs opened up the classroom. Making chairs independent of each other allowed a freedom and access that didn't exist with the old

RANDOM THOUGHTS ON UNIVERSAL DESIGN

With access comes responsibility

Bruce Hannah

tied-together chair. Thinking of the student as an independent learner was a big physical and metaphorical step.

Schools are complicated, messy environments that reflect the community which they serve. Schools are miniature towns and reflect the mores and ethics of the community in which they exist. If a community is accessible probably the schools in it will also be accessible. Using the school building and grounds as a model for an ideal town can help in educating the students about access.

A school building usually consists of a series of classrooms, a library, gymnasium, music room, art room, and offices. Most even have a medical facility, connected by halls, stairs, ramps, and elevators. Every condition that might occur in a small town can occur in a high school or on a college campus. In fact, the campus might even be more complex. The addition of a stadium creates a small town. Purdue University in Indiana has attempted to create an accessible campus.

Learning environments take many forms, some are reconstructions of living and working environments designed to simulate actual places and spaces. These serve to rehabilitate and reeducate people who are recovering from disabling experiences, but we might learn something about ordinary environments by studying these. Patrcia Moore and David Guynes design rehabilitation environments and products for the elderly, the disabled, and everybody else. Independence Square Rehabilitation Centers, designed and produced by Guynes Design Inc. (GDI), are installed across the United States. Each center recreates a wide range of typical urban and suburban spaces and places that will be encountered in real world situations. The controlled setting lets a person recovering from illness or injury relearn and practice the basic activities of daily life, like shopping, dining out, climbing out of a car, or crossing a street.

Attention to details as minute as sidewalk cracks, gravel, grass, curb cuts, and the stairs into the delicatessen re-recreate not only the dreamed-of Accessible Utopia, but also the obstacles one will encounter walking down the street. Re-recreated in the style of the region, each center mirrors the actual conditions the disabled will encounter—ATMs, cafes, theaters, and transportation such as buses, cars, or subways. Everything about the environment reflects the community, down to names on the stores and businesses. (*Courtesy of Guynes Design Incorporated.*)

Figure 5.1 **Our Town Market Rehabilitation Center. Designed by GDI.**

Space: Rehab Scenario

By recreating the check-out counter in Our Town, GDI helps rehabilitate people who are newly disabled. It provides practical experience without the embarrassment, or danger, of attempting to deal with real life situations. (*Courtesy of Guynes Design Incorporated.*)

Space: Rehab Scenario

Recreating the street in Our Town with all the obstacles one encounters—including curbs, sidewalks, mailboxes, and

Figure 5.2 **Our Town Street Rehabilitation Center. Designed by GDI.**

street furniture—GDI helps rehabilitate the disabled with ease and teach confidence that helps create a feeling of independence. (*Courtesy of Guynes Design Incorporated.*)

Space: Rehab Scenario

Main Street reintroduces real scenarios as the recently disabled learns mobility skills. (*Courtesy of Guynes Design Incorporated.*)

Figure 5.3 **Main Street Rehabilitation Center. Designed by GDI.**

RANDOM THOUGHTS ON UNIVERSAL DESIGN

What is Universal Design? A product or place which greets every person with an embrace, embodies universality. Judging all people and their individual needs as equal by design.

Patricia A. Moore

Space: Rehab Scenario

A unique approach to the design of pediatric rehabilitation centers utilizing an interactive concept. Configured as a life-size board game featuring Mr. Pipes control station, children are able to accomplish skill-building training. (*Courtesy of Guynes Design Incorporated.*)

Figure 5.4 **"Rehab 123" Rehabilitation Center. Designed by GDI.**

Space: Rehab Scenario

Another unique approach to the design of pediatric rehabilitation centers utilizing an interactive concept. Notice how toys are set at different height levels for easy access,

Figure 5.5 **"Rehab 123" Rehabilitation Center Designed by GDI.**

and learning boards are created with large lettering, related pictures, and vibrant colors. (*Courtesy of Guynes Design Incorporated.*)

Figure 5.6 **American Museum of Natural History—Dinosaur Exhibit, 1995. Ralph Appelbaum Associates, "Touch Fossils." (***Photo: © Scott Frances, ESTO***)**

Space: Museum Scenario

For the fossil halls at the American Museum of Natural History, RAA included universal accessibility with interactives and graphics, close-captioning on audio-visual productions, and lifts to certain interpretive experiences. (*Courtesy of Ralph Appelbaum Associates.*)

RANDOM THOUGHTS ON UNIVERSAL DESIGN

In the early eighties I visited a museum exhibit of modern sculpture. This exhibit was billed as a touch exhibit "for the blind." I attended with a sighted friend and a fellow legally blind advocate. My visually impaired acquaintance and I used neither canes nor dogs at that time. The exhibit was partially funded by the NEA [National Endowment for the Arts] and I had been asked to visit the site for evaluation in the capacity as an advocate.

There were a number of interesting pieces including a large ribbon sculpture made from coils of inch-thick rope. As my visually impaired friend and I leaned over the ribbon of rope sculpture, bracing our elbows on it to better read the hand printed sign pasted on the wall behind it, my sighted friend came up behind us and said, "The sign says DON'T LEAN ON THE SCULPTURE." I think the exhibit designer had missed a vital point.

George Covington

Space: Museum Scenario

For the fossil halls at the American Museum of Natural History, RAA included touch fossil stations to encourage children and facilitate understanding. Close-captioning on video programs provides an alternative to sound. (*Courtesy of Ralph Appelbaum Associates.*)

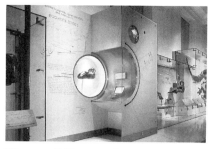

Figure 5.7 **American Museum of Natural History—Dinosaur Exhibit, "Info. Stations." 1995. Ralph Appelbaum Associates. (*Photo: © Scott Frances, ESTO*)**

RANDOM THOUGHTS ON UNIVERSAL DESIGN

Concern and accommodation have always been mandates at [Ralph Applebaum Associates] and we aim to create seemless accessibility as a natural element in our design. We have incorporated braille Signage [and] audio and family labels at the Rochester Museum & Science Center, and wheelchair accessibility to all media at the United States Holocaust Memorial Museum. We also created privacy walls in the Holocaust installation to shield children and others from sensitive material.

For the fossil halls at the American Museum of Natural History, we included universal accessibility to interactives and graphics, close-captioning on audio-visual productions, lifts to certain interpretive experiences, and fossils to engage children and facilitate understanding for the visually impaired and other visitors.

At the Japanese-American National Museum in Los Angeles, we created "remembrance books" in which Japanese-American visitors who were interned in American concentration camps during World War II may record their experiences—a unique cross-cultural and cross-generational invitation.

Ralph Appelbaum Associates

Space: Museum Scenario

Braille labels and audio programs are alongside traditional graphic panels. This illustrates how providing many forms of communication in museums builds "bridges" to the exhibits. (*Courtesy of Ralph Appelbaum Associates.*)

Figure 5.8 **"At the Western Door" an exhibit at the Rochester Museum and History Science Center. Designed by Ralph Appelbaum Associates.**

Space: Museum Scenario

This aims to provide an understanding of the magnitude of the Holocaust using a mass of photographs with the use of architecture and light. (*Courtesy Ralph of Appelbaum Associates.*)

Figure 5.9 **"Iconic Tower" of Photos at the United States Holocaust Memorial Museum in Washington, DC. Designed by Ralph Appelbaum Associates. (*Photo: © Timothy Hursley*)**

Space: Museum Scenario

Narrative photographs create visual storytelling sequences.
(*Courtesy Ralph of Appelbaum Associates.*)

Figure 5.10 **"Liberation 1945" at the United States Holocaust Memorial Museum in Washington, DC. Designed by Ralph Appelbaum Associates. (*Photo: Christopher Micelli*)**

Space: Museum Scenario

Ramps in the museum become part of the interpretive experience. (*Courtesy Ralph of Appelbaum Associates.*)

Figure 5.11 **Air Navigation Gallery at the National Science and Technology Museum of Taiwan. Designed by Ralph Appelbaum Associates. (*Photo: Eli Kuslansky*)**

"Universal Design is a vision of creating public and cultural edifices that acknowledge demographic reality. It is a design of inclusion and accommodation, generous in spirit and concerned in detail.

"As a culture, we are entering a new maturity, one which does not and can not, in all conscience, shrink from the examination of difficult subjects and painful truths. Correlative to this is the realization that the world is as it is and does not conform to any abstract norm. In order to function as valid cultural institutions, museums must address the wide needs and various physical and intellectual capabilities of their visitors. This requires design for varieties of communication and provision for accessibility—pansocietally. Anything less constitutes a default of cultural responsibility.

"The foundation of a concept of Universal Design is the acknowledgement of a simple truth: that all of us, regardless of age or condition, make up the fabric of society, and the function of design is to render circumstances amenable to a wide diversity of needs as a matter of course."

Ralph Appelbaum
Founder
Ralph Appelbaum Associates

Figure 5.12 **Optelec 20/20 Spectrum Color Video Magnification System.**

Product: Video Magnification System

The 20/20 Spectrum is a high-quality video magnification system designed to satisfy the needs of visually impaired persons at work or school. It magnifies from 5 to 60 times. It is height adjustable and the screen tilts to accommodate different viewing angles. (*Courtesy of Optelec U.S. Inc., 6 Liberty Way, Westford, MA 01886.*)

Product: Magnification Software

With LP-DOS computer graphics, text and animation can be magnified up to 16 times, allowing complete access to a computer's applications. (*Courtesy of Optelec U.S. Inc., 6 Liberty Way, Westford, MA 01886.*)

Figure 5.13 **Optelec LP-DOS Magnification Software.**

SCHOOL TRANSITIONS TO REMEMBER

Transitions from one space, service, or product to another often present barriers whether physical or psychological.

1. Threshold Access: School Entrance; Doors

2. Vertical Assent: Stairs; Elevator; Escalator

3. Classroom Access

4. Cafeteria Access: Counters; Chairs; Tables

5. Gym Access: Facilities

6. Auditorium Access

7. Library and Media Center Access

8. Restroom Access: Doorways; Fixtures; Facilities

9. Technological Access; Communications; Computers

10. Art and Music Access

11. Shop and Kitchen Access

12. Outdoor Access; Play Areas and Fields

CHECK LIST
Accessible School

1. Remember—adults go to school also.

2. Schools are used 24 hours a day.

3. Teaching access begins by setting examples.

4. Playgrounds and gyms are places of equality.

5. Art and design are taught to everyone.

6. Simple, intuitive information. Intuitive use is paramount to understanding.

7. Signage is for everyone in the school.

8. Can the students *hear* the information?

9. Can the students *see* the information?

10. Can the students *touch* the information?

CHAPTER 6

THE STADIUM AND SPORTS

The phrase "level playing field" becomes more meaningful as sports become more and more accessible, and gender barriers continue to fall as competition between the sexes gets closer. The Special Olympics made everyone aware of the individual capabilities and enthusiasm we all have for sports and the shared rewards of competition. Access to playing fields, courts, and arenas lets everyone test their own limits and abilities. The joy of being a spectator or player is a shared communal experience that reinforces our joy in sports.

Space: Stadium Scenario

Ramped level changes and convertible seating for wheelchair users, in this accessible stadium, were key ingredients in making Oriole Park at Camden Yards accessible. Winner of a National Accessibility Award and an AIA Honor Award, Oriole Park makes the playing field a little more "on the level."

Designed by HOK this facility seamlessly permits accessibility. The ramps are used by everyone; the seats are used by everyone; ticket windows are accessible to everyone; and

Figure 6.1 **Ramp Levels in Oriole Park at Camden Yards. Designed by HOK Architects.**

water fountains, restrooms, and sky boxes are accessible. Sports are available to everyone. Entertainment shouldn't be a chore. By incorporating everyone into the joy and beauty of the game HOK made baseball fun again. Assisted-listening devices for the hearing impaired make listening to the game easy. Oriole Park challenges the idea of "separate but equal." Both physically and intellectually. It sets a new standard to be met or exceeded. *(Courtesy of Hellmuth, Obata, & Kassabaum, Inc.)*

RANDOM THOUGHTS ON UNIVERSAL DESIGN

"It's a way of thinking; a new ingredient to design education and professional practice that can become a catalyst for invigorating our design sensibilities."

Bill Palmer
HOK Architect

Space: Stadium Scenario

What better way to celebrate accessibility than by a baseball game played in an accessible arena? *(Courtesy of Hellmuth, Obata, & Kassabaum, Inc.)*

Figure 6.2 **Opening Day Ceremonies**

RANDOM THOUGHTS ON UNIVERSAL DESIGN

"People with disabilities help to point out difficulties in the built environment that others take for granted and can easily over come. Products and environments designed for accessibility ultimately make life easier for all of us."

Kim Beasley
Paradigm Design Group

Stadium Seating

This sketch of the accessible stadium seat demonstrates how each seat can be raised and pivoted out of the way to make room for a wheelchair. *(Courtesy of Kim Beasley.)*

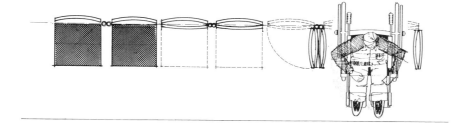

Figure 6.3 Sketch of Accessible Stadium Seating. Designed by Kim Beasley.

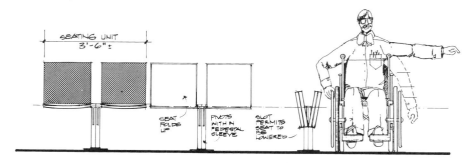

Stadium Seating

As each seat is pivoted out of the way to make room for a wheelchair, it occupies only the space under the arm leaving the area free to operate the wheelchair. *(Courtesy of Kim Beasley.)*

Figure 6.4 Model of Accessible Stadium Seating. Designed by Kim Beasley.

Figure 6.5 **Accessible Stadium Seating. Designed by Kim Beasley.**

Stadium Seating

Making stadiums accessible to wheelchairs was Kim Beasley's goal when designing this stadium seat. The design makes it possible for anyone in a wheelchair to sit anywhere along an accessible route. The model demonstrates how each seat can be raised and pivoted out of the way to make room for a wheelchair. *(Courtesy of Kim Beasley.)*

Concept: Way Finding

Conceived by Kim Beasley, Paradigm Design Group, ADA consultants to the Atlanta Committee for the Olympic Games. An aid to "see" with your hands. The model was built by Kevin Williams while he was a student at Pratt Institute. Remember the old admonition, "You see with your eyes and not with your hands," well, Paradigm Design Group has turned the idea upside down and created a model that is designed to be touched. Aiding in the ability

Figure 6.6 **Tactile Model 1996 Olympics, Atlanta.**

to locate where events are located in the Olympic stadium. *(Courtesy of Kim Beasley.)*

Concept: Way Finding
Conceived by Kim Beasley, Paradigm Design Group, ADA consultants to the 1996 Atlanta Olympic Games. The model is also an orientation tool used to allow blind and visually impaired people to understand the design, layout, and scale of the stadium. *(Courtesy of Kim Beasley.)*

Figure 6.7 **1996 Olympics, Atlanta.**

Concept: Way Finding
Once the site of an event is located on the model it's very easy to translate that into a visual projection in the Olympic stadium. *(Courtesy of Kim Beasley.)*

Figure 6.8 **1996 Olympics, Atlanta.**

STADIUM AND SPORTS TRANSITIONS TO REMEMBER

Transitions from one space, service, or product to another often present barriers whether physical or psychological.

1. Parking Access

2. Threshold Access: Entrance; Doors

3. Vertical Assent: Stairs, Elevator, Escalator

4. Ticket Access

5. Gift Shop Access

6. Seat Access

7. Field Access

8. Food Stands Access

9. Restroom Access: Doorways; Fixtures; Facilities

10. Technological Access: Communications; Computers

11. Fishing

CHECK LIST

Accessible Sports

1. **Is arriving at the sporting event made easy? Is parking easy and accessible? Is public transportation easy and accessible?**

2. **Is buying a ticket easy?**

3. **Getting to your seat should be easy. Are seats and sky boxes accessible? Can wheelchair users be accommodated?**

4. **Buying drinks, peanuts, popcorn, and Cracker Jack should be accessible and easy.**

5. **Are assisted-listening devices available?**

6. **Are water fountains and restrooms accessible for everyone?**

7. **Is the Signage clearly laid out, for both visual and tactile "reading"?**

CHAPTER 7

COMMUNICATIONS AND MEDIA

Being able to communicate anywhere, anytime has been a long-proposed dream of many futurists and science fiction writers. *Star Trek* introduced us to the flip phone concept when Captain Kirk commanded Scotty to "beam us up!" Dick Tracy's wrist radio was yet another dream idea that recently became a reality. Personal communicators, whether they are flip phones, wrist radios, or medical emergency devices, are universal in their design and breed independence. They provide safety and security and encourage people to explore; they are playful in their approach to communication. From the individual who can safely wander about his or her own home to the wilderness explorer, the technology frees us from the tethers long associated with communication, cords, and cables. Products that roam freely and services that compress the technology into manageable, understandable bytes are available and are changing how we live and work.

Voice dialing is a "back to the future" service that restores the simple scenario long played out in rural America when phone companies relied on operators to connect callers. At that time, it was the norm to pick up the phone and have the operator ask "number please" and, if for ex-

Figure 7.1 **Motorola's MicroTAC Digital Elite Cellular Telephone.**

ample, you wanted to speak to your dad, the operator knew who you were and where your dad worked and you were connected to him immediately. A simple, elegant solution to communication, which is now called voice dialing, eliminating the need to remember a number or even a code button. A truly Universal idea has returned.

Phones

A cellular phone is a convenience for all, especially people in wheelchairs or with reduced mobility. This product's optional vibration alert mode also makes it useful for hearing-impaired people. It's light enough to be easily carried in a pocket, has a built-in answering machine, and has an optional headset for cord-free and hands-free use. (*Courtesy of Motorola, Inc.*)

Phones

The Big Button Plus Telephone has extra-large buttons with concave "wells" designed to help people "target" the buttons. (*Courtesy of Henry Dreyfuss Associates.*)

Figure 7.2 **AT&T Big-Button Plus Telephone. Designed by Henry Dreyfuss Associates for AT&T.**

Phones

Starting with the architecture of the ergonomic handset, the phone was designed with input from real-life users. The designers were most concerned with the ear comfort around the speaker, the hand grip, and the dialing ability whether one handed, left handed, or right handed. By using thermal-sensitive paint on handset contours that graded highly in use tests, the design team was able to photograph "pressure maps" of a thermal imprint left after use. These thermal imprints lead the team to three principles that guided their handset design.

1. The majority of handset users extended their index finger because of a lack of a place to close it around the phone. This was alleviated by "bulging" the bottom of the handset.

2. The bulge also created a taper that helped fill the palm and gave a more comfortable grip. The tapered form allows it to stand up.

3. A soft ridge on the side of the phone creates a place for the fingers to rest so that they don't wrap around the phone body and grip the button area. (*Courtesy of Sony Corporation of America.*)

Figure 7.3 **Sony Cordless Digital Answering Machine/Telephone. Designed by the Sony Corporation of America Design Center.**

Phones

The Jog Shuttle control concept uses the intuitive metaphor of the "analog dial," or wheel, to clearly present all the playback functions in one easily understood control. Instead of a series of buttons to push or click, the user simply turns the easily gripped control wheel either right or left to either speed up or slow down the playback, as well as record, erase, rewind, or skip forward or backward to important messages. (*Courtesy of Sony Corporation of America.*)

Figure 7.4 **Sony Cordless Digital Answering Machine/Telephone (Jog Shuttle). Designed by the Sony Corporation of America Design Center.**

Figure 7.5 **Dictaphone: Passport Digital Portable (PDA).**

Dictaphones

The Dictaphone PDA is a personal organizational tool. A verbal notepad, an answering machine, a transcription recorder, a message taker and leaver, a voice mail system all in one device. The user is given the capability of several machines without the cords or needing the machines themselves. This rather simple idea has become very important in the age of information. (*Courtesy of Dictaphone.*)

Dictaphones

This is designed to accommodate both handheld and microphone input, plus it has intercom capabilities. The vertical free-standing concept has a small footprint which occupies a small amount of deskspace and is easy to use. (*Courtesy of Dictaphone.*)

Figure 7.6 **Dictaphone: Voice Processor.**

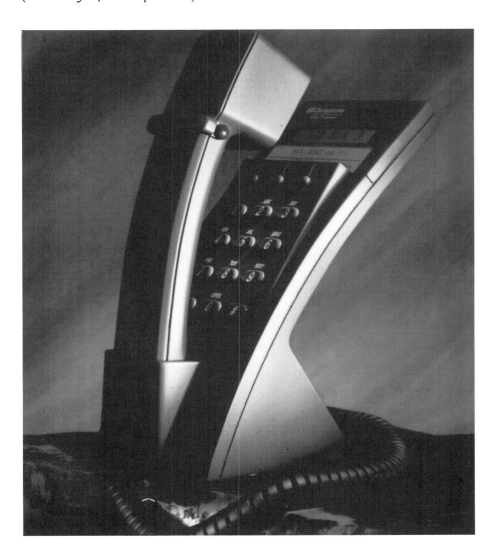

Dictaphones

This is designed to accommodate both handheld and microphone input and has intercom capabilities. The adjustable LCD screen displays selected functions in easy-to-read, nonglare lettering. The optional hand microphone has a bar code scanner and LCD display built into it. (*Courtesy of Dictaphone.*)

Figure 7.7 **Dictaphone: Digital Connections.**

Product: Wristwatch

Designed and manufactured by Timex. These watches were designed in response to consumer requests for "A watch I can read" that is fashionable and stylish. The watches combine easy-to-read white dials with full Arabic numerals in black and black hands that are wider than normal, for easy reading at a glance. Removal of the minute track on some styles makes the numbers even easier to read. (*Courtesy of Timex.*)

Figure 7.8 **Timex Easy Reader Watches.**

Media

Two-way TV is a system that enables subscribers to interact directly with broadcast programs in real time. The handset is used with a graphic interface superimposed on the broadcast image. (*Courtesy of Geoff Hollington Associates.*)

Figure 7.9 **Two-Way TV Handset. Designed by Geoff Hollington with Peter Emrys-Roberts, Hollington Associates for the Two-Way TV company.**

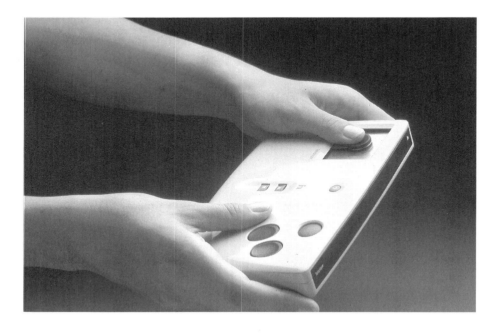

Figure 7.10 **VoicePrint by Qualex Inc. Designed by Tanaka Kapec.**

Media

The VoicePrint is an interactive photograph in a special mount that allows the user to record and play back a personal message. (*Courtesy of Kenro Izu.*)

RANDOM THOUGHTS ON UNIVERSAL DESIGN

"Universal Design is the concept of designing products so that anyone can use them. In practice, I believe products should be designed so that anyone who is **likely** to use a product should find it easy to do so, regardless of their abilities or disabilities."

Ken Schory
Director of Industrial Design
AT&T Global Information Systems

Product: Assisted Hearing Device

This is a conceptual product intended to facilitate communication between deaf and hearing individuals. It uses "biphasic waves," electromagnetic impulses given off by muscles as they extend and contract to translate gestures into words. Wristwatch-like sensors gather gesture information and deliver the translated words through small speakers. (*Courtesy of AT&T.*)

Figure 7.11 **Communication Device for the Hearing Impaired. Designed by Dylan Jobe, a student at the Center for Creative Studies while a summer intern at AT&T's Design Center in 1994.**

Concept: Personal Digital Assistant

The Dove combines the user attributes of a cellular phone, synthesized speech-assisted device, personal digital assistant, and a notebook computer, using voice as the primary interface medium. It offers voice and handwriting recognition, wireless networking, and communication combined with multiple flat panel displays. In most interactions information is displayed visually **and** audibly and reinforced by animation, promoting universal use. (*Courtesy of Fitch Inc.*)

Figure 7.12 **Digital Equipment Corporation's Dove, a Next-Generation Personal Digital Assistant (PDA). Designed by Fitch Inc.**

Concept: Personal Digital Assistant

The physical design maximizes flexibility. Sliding open a panel exposes a small panel useful in walking or driving situations. Dove communicates its active status with a clock that also highlights important events with dots at appointment times. (*Courtesy of Fitch Inc.*)

Figure 7.13 Digital Equipment Corporation's Dove, a Next-Generation Personal Digital Assistant (PDA). Designed by Fitch Inc.

Figure 7.14 Digital Equipment Corporation's Dove, a Next-Generation Personal Digital Assistant (PDA). Designed by Fitch Inc.

Concept: Personal Digital Assistant

A track pad and stylus screen module allows pen–pad input. (*Courtesy of Fitch Inc.*)

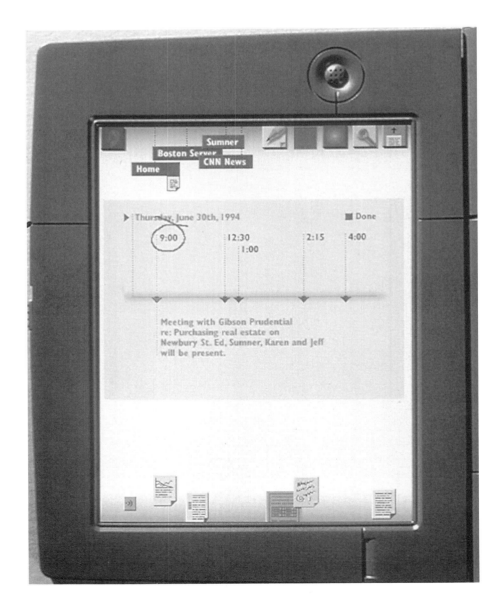

Concept: Personal Digital Assistant

In addition to its many other features, the Dove computer, with its traditional keyboard, serves as an excellent notebook for recording messages. (*Courtesy of Fitch Inc.*)

Figure 7.15 **Digital Equipment Corporation's Dove, a Next-Generation Personal Digital Assistant (PDA). Designed by Fitch Inc.**

COMMUNICATIONS AND MEDIA TRANSITIONS TO REMEMBER

Transitions from one space, service, or product to another often present barriers whether physical or psychological.

1. Phone Access: TDX; TDD

2. Fax Access

3. Copier Access

4. Computer Access

5. Internet Access

6. Mail Access

7. Television Access: Close-captioning

8. Radio Access

9. VCR Access: Programming Services

CHECK LIST
Accessible Media

1. Use more than one sense to communicate—be redundant. Develop high contrast between control buttons, levers, etc. and control panels.

2. Use bells that ring at different frequencies and volumes to help identify different phones or communication devices.

3. Use visual signalers such as flashing lights or lamps to increase the ability to respond to calls or messages.

4. Make signals vibrate, for privacy.

5. Use amplification devices for telephones and headsets to allow the user to adjust the volume.

6. Use large, simple, sans serf typefaces.

7. Back up everything with braille.

8. LCD readouts sometimes need analog support.

9. Voice activation is a reality.

10. Eliminate unnecessary controls such as on/off switches if possible.

11. Make actions intuitive.

12. Assure software/hardware compatibility, or design it as one product.

13. Is the telephone handset ergonomically designed? Can the phone be dialed one handed?

14. Are remote controls easy to operate with large buttons? Are the functions easy to see, with high-contrast colors or the use of textures?

CHAPTER 8

THE ROAD AND TRAVELING

"While attending a design conference," remembers Bruce Hannah, "I happened to sit between a pair of industrialists during a presentation by an automobile designer. The presentation was about the future, when we [could] get into our car and verbally instruct it where to go. As the presentation was ending, one of the industrialists turned to the other and said, 'We have that now, all we do is ask Mark to take us to Atlantic City.'"

Access sometimes is already available—it's the price that keeps us from using it. Access to transportation is one of the most coveted aspects of American society. Too often people with disabilities have been left out of the mobility equation in both private and public transportation. By using all the senses to inform passengers of destinations and stops, transportation becomes more accessible to everyone.

Travel is now a way of life—we get on and off planes, trains, and automobiles without thinking twice. Traveling between cities is a daily occurrence for many people. Holidays spent jetting around the world are second nature, but as our population ages, accessibility to travel becomes more critical. There is a growing need to accommodate this aging Baby Boomer population. Hoteliers and travel experts understand it's good business to make travel accessible to everyone.

Combine the ability to access information individually on a global scale with portable computers and a new kind of traveler emerges. A nomad in touch all the time.

Figure 8.1 **The Talking Bus by Digital Recorders, Inc.**

Product: Digital Voice Messages

The Talking Bus is an on-vehicle message and passenger information system that announces all stops, transfers, and intersections of public transportation systems. This makes transportation more accessible and safer. It also helps tourists who don't read English. (*Courtesy of Digital Recorders, Inc.*)

Product: Digital Voice Messages

These are voice messaging systems used by highway travel advisors to alert motorists and travelers of changing conditions. Reports are broadcast over low-power AM radio stations to inform travelers of weather conditions, construc-

Figure 8.2 **Highway Advisory Radio Systems by Digital Recorders, Inc.**

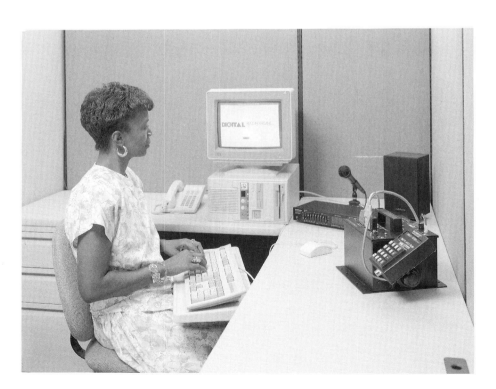

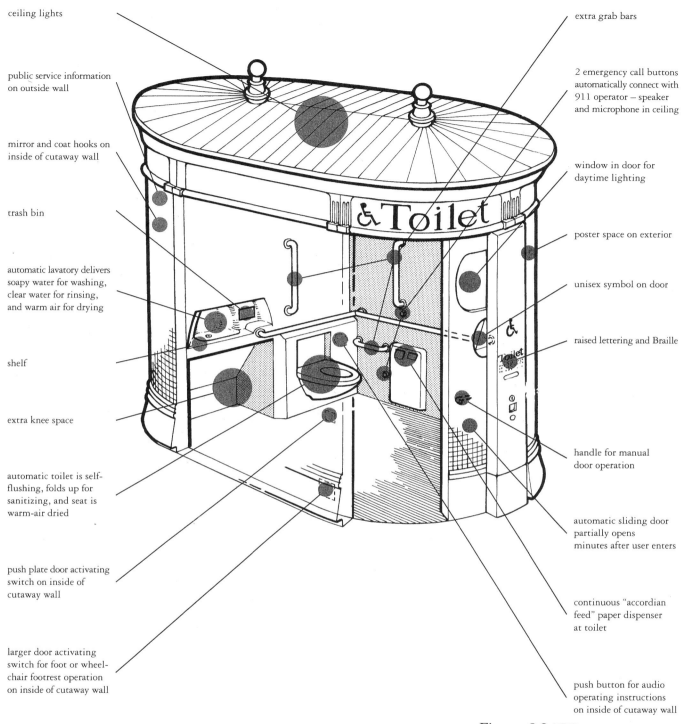

ceiling lights

public service information
on outside wall

mirror and coat hooks on
inside of cutaway wall

trash bin

automatic lavatory delivers
soapy water for washing,
clear water for rinsing,
and warm air for drying

shelf

extra knee space

automatic toilet is self-
flushing, folds up for
sanitizing, and seat is
warm-air dried

push plate door activating
switch on inside of
cutaway wall

larger door activating
switch for foot or wheel-
chair footrest operation
on inside of cutaway wall

extra grab bars

2 emergency call buttons
automatically connect with
911 operator – speaker
and microphone in ceiling

window in door for
daytime lighting

poster space on exterior

unisex symbol on door

raised lettering and Braille

handle for manual
door operation

automatic sliding door
partially opens
minutes after user enters

continuous "accordian
feed" paper dispenser
at toilet

push button for audio
operating instructions
on inside of cutaway wall

Figure 8.3 **JCDecaux
Automatic Public Toilet.**

tion delays, and alternate routes. All of this makes safer and
more accessible travel. (*Courtesy of Digital Recorders, Inc.*)

Street Restroom

Street furniture that is accessible was the design goal set by
JCDecaux when developing its latest toilet, in consultation
with Accessible Environments and Barrier Free Environ-

ments. It exceeds all the regulations set by the ADA. All of the amenities around the toilet have been carefully selected and developed into an accessibility system that is flexible and provides a range of options to the user. By starting with the wheelchair user as their focus JCDecaux created a toilet accessible to all. A simple idea such as using accordion-fold toilet paper, because it dispenses from a flush-wall fitting, frees up wall space to accommodate a grab bar. The schematic drawing illustrates all the features that create an accessible street toilet. (*Courtesy of JCDecaux.*)

Figure 8.4 **JCDecaux Toilet.**

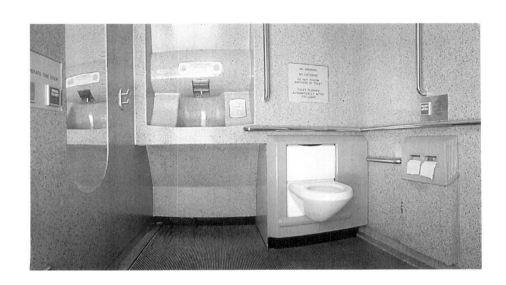

Street Restroom

The features of this toilet include push-button audio operating instructions, natural lighting supplemented by ceiling lights, and an automatic toilet that self-flushes and cleans after every use (the seat is sanitized and air dried). (*Courtesy of JCDecaux.*)

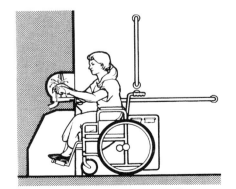

Figure 8.5 **JCDecaux Toilet. The State-of-the-Art Sink.**

Street Restroom

By simply placing your hands under the tap, water and soap are dispensed. The warm-air dryer comes on automatically when the water stops flowing. The recess under the sink accommodates the widest range of adaptive equipment. Located on the wall and floor are buttons which activate an emergency call system and automatically call 911. The operator communicates through a built-in speaker and microphone. The door opens automatically after 20 minutes or can be activated by buttons located at the doorway and at floor level. The JCDecaux automatic public toilet maintains high design and accessibility goals. (*Courtesy of JCDecaux.*)

RANDOM THOUGHTS ON UNIVERSAL DESIGN

"Universal accessibility to space and information is an act of love that designers give to society."

Fred Blumlien

SIGNAGE

Directing people to the destination and highlighting the important stopping off points is the role of Signage. As the world becomes more accessible Signage plays a larger role in just getting around. The ADA requires that architectural and communication barriers be removed from existing public accommodations. Hotels, hospitals, restaurants, banks, movie theaters, libraries, schools, museums, airports, convention centers, factories, stores warehouses, and office buildings need accessible Signage.

There are a few guidelines that can be followed that can make Signage more accessible. Colors, writing, and/or symbols should be in high contrast to the basic sign color. The background must be matte or other nonglare surface. Braille and other tactile characters must be raised a minimum of 1/32nd of an inch and be of Grade 2 braille.

Characters must be in uppercase and sans serif. Tactile characters must be a minimum of 5/8 inch and a maximum of 2 inches high. Characters on overhead signs should be a minimum of 3 inches high.

Figure 8.6 **International Symbol of Accessibility.**

Concept: General Signage

When there is more than one entrance to a building, the international symbol of accessibility is used to identify accessible entrances. (*Courtesy of System 2/90, Inc.*)

RANDOM THOUGHTS ON UNIVERSAL DESIGN

Why do we limit our vocabulary of Signage to stick figures and geometric shapes? The visual vocabulary for "man" and "woman" alone is quite extensive, ranging from the Greek symbols used in medicine, to the moon for woman and the sun for man, to Giacometi's slender male figures, and Titian's fully formed woman. People can carry around more than one idea. Everytime a new cave is discovered with yet-older art, scientists are shocked at the sophistication of the drawings. Why? Because prehistoric man is incapable of expressing thoughts in written words and only pictures? Perhaps the scientists expect to eventually find stick figures that will prove the dumbness of the root humanoids. I doubt it will ever happen. Human beings are extremely visually, complex animals, seeing images with a clarity and purpose that can defy the imagination. The visual vocabulary that most people are capable of is probably shrinking because we are subjected to less variation and visual diversity every day. Prehistoric people depended on their visions to express wide ranges of behavior and content. Something graphic designers are just beginning to reunderstand.

Bruce Hannah

Concept: General Signage

If a facility has a public text telephone this symbol identifies it. (*Courtesy of System 2/90, Inc.*)

Figure 8.7 **International TDD Symbol for Text Telephones.**

Concept: General Signage

Assisted listening systems are identified by this symbol. (*Courtesy of System 2/90, Inc.*)

Concept: General Signage

System 2/90 is based on three basic components; a rail, an insert, and end caps. From these three components an infi-

Figure 8.8 **International Symbol for Hearing Loss.**

Figure 8.9 **System 2/90: A Flexible Response to the Demand for Modular Signage.**

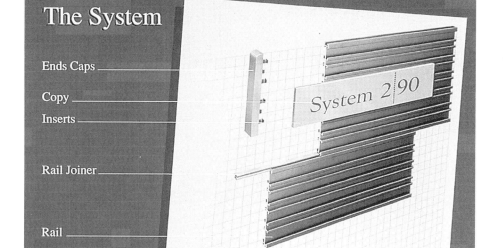

nite variety of configurations can be created. And any one of these configurations can accommodate another infinite variety of identities, messages, and functions, including braille. (*Courtesy of System 2/90, Inc.*)

Concept: General Signage

Signs that designate permanent rooms should include tactile and braille lettering. (*Courtesy of System 2/90, Inc.*)

Figure 8.10 **System 2/90 Modular Facility Signage.**

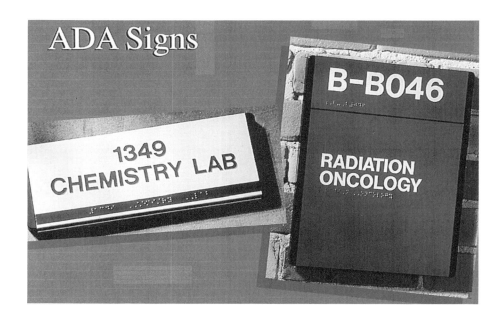

Concept: General Signage

Some parts of a sign, such as a name, time, and date are temporary and are interchangeable. (*Courtesy of System 2/90, Inc.*)

Figure 8.11 **System 2/90 Modular Facility Signage.**

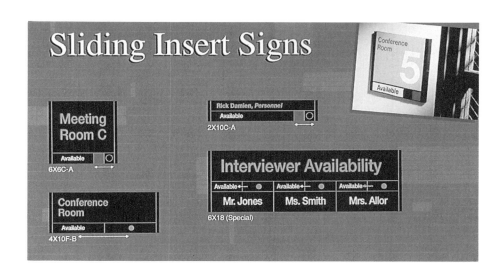

Concept: General Signage

Exterior Signage indicates where a person is ("You are here") and shows a route or routes to a desired destination, using the mapped layout of the area. (*Courtesy of System 2/90, Inc.*)

Figure 8.12 **System 2/90 Modular Facility Signage.**

Concept: General Signage

Finding the location of the poop deck or the orlop deck, as shown indicated in many languages, could prove to be a learning experience. (*Courtesy of System 2/90, Inc.*)

Figure 8.13 **System 2/90 Modular Facility Signage.**

Concept: General Signage

Movable Signage adds to the flexibility of a Signage system. (*Courtesy of System 2/90, Inc.*)

Figure 8.14 **System 2/90 Modular Facility Signage.**

As we travel about places whether they are cities or rural lanes we are made acutely aware of where we are by all of our senses. The glare of a light, the crash of a can, the crunching of rustling leaves beneath our feet, the aroma of garlic, the spray of salt air all add up to the image of a place. All senses play their role in our definition of place. Some of this richness is being reevaluated and restated as designers become more aware of the phenomena of way finding, a complex mixture of sight, sound, smell, touch, taste, and kinesthetics.

A few years ago when my youngest daughter first traveled from New York to Los Angeles by plane her senses were tricked by design. We arrived at Newark Airport justifiably early to give us enough time to acclimate our daughter to the concept of air travel. She roamed around the airport investigating and observing, as any curious three-year-old will do. Eventually we boarded the plane and flew for the interminable five or six hours.

Before deplaning we told Lizzie we had arrived in Los Angeles and she would soon see her grandmother. As we left the plane Lizzie burst into tears, declaring that we were still in Newark; we had played a cruel joke on her, we had never left Newark. Trying to explain to a three-year-old that all airline terminals looked the same, no matter where you went, wouldn't do. She believed her eyes, not the Signage. Design had failed. The graphic designers and way finders are facing a formidable task to reinvent Signage so that we intuitively know where we are.

Bruce Hannah

GRAPHICS—NEW YORK CITY SUBWAY SIGNAGE INVESTIGATION

The design team consisted of Louis Nelson at Louis Nelson Associates, Sam Lebowitz at Lebowitz/Gould, and Lance Wyman and Roger Whitehouse at Wyman/Whitehouse. Their directive was to review the Signage and communications systems and make recommendations for a Communication Design and Way Finding Project for New York City's Metropolitan Transit Authority. Enriching the vocabularies used to communicate in the subway by historical and vernacular references, along with the clarification of goals of the project, led to the following visual presentation.

Concept: Subway Signage Goals

· Reestablishing the meaning of the color yellow as a warning

· Change the transfer signs

· Use a less-aggressive arrow

· Make matte black beautiful

· Eliminate glare

· Make the entrances visible

· Separate advertising from direction signs

· Bring light to darkness

· Eliminate fear

· Eliminate disinformation (*Courtesy of NY Transit.*)

Concept: Subway Signage

The goal was to define stations by creating a rich visual vocabulary that reflects the individual and unique architectural and community of important stations. Times Square is different from Union Square. A rider will immediately be

Re-establish the meaning of the color yellow.

Change the transfer signs.

Use a less aggressive arrow.

Make mat black beautiful.

Eliminate glare.

Make the entrances visible.

Separate advertising from directional signs.

Bring light to darkness.

Eliminate fear.

Eliminate disinformation.

Figure 8.15 **NY Transit #1.**

Figure 8.16 **NY Transit #3.**

Figure 8.17 **NY Transit #4.**

aware of where they are by the visual clues presented in the Signage and also by the distinctive atmosphere of each station. In the New York City subway system there is a heritage of visual clues incorporated in the original tile work of the stations. Astor Place is identified by a beaver, recalling the fur trading of the Astor family. Fulton Street is identified by a steamboat to honor Robert Fulton, who pioneered the steamboat.

These visualizations give the passenger instant information whether or not they can read English. They enrich the experience of riding the subway and provide historical information, also. (*Courtesy of NY Transit.*)

Concept: Subway Signage
Test graphic of a typical station sign to determine what can be easily read. Specifically, the sign tested for legibility, readability, and confirmation of location. (*Courtesy of NY Transit.*)

Questions most asked by Riders

· Where is the Subway?

· Is this the right train?

- How do I pay?

- Where is my train?

- Does this train go to my stop?

- Is this my stop?

- Where is the right exit?

- How do I get to my destination?

Concept: Subway Signage

Illustration of braille way finding concept placed outside the entrances to the subway. (*Courtesy of NY Transit.*)

Figure 8.18 **NY Transit #6.**

Concept: Subway Signage

A compass depicted on the ground. Understanding that people need to be oriented in order to take advantage of directions, the Transit Authority came up with this plain and logical solution to a basic problem, something that every city and town should provide. (*Courtesy of NY Transit.*)

Figure 8.19 **NY Transit #7.**

Concept: Subway Signage

This enhances the visual information by using existing structures and adding appropriate graphics. This is a vocabulary of visual clues developed from the historical and cultural information of each site. The clues are meant to comfort and lead the passengers, to reassure the passengers that they are where they want to be. (*Courtesy of NY Transit.*)

Figure 8.20 **NY Transit #8.**

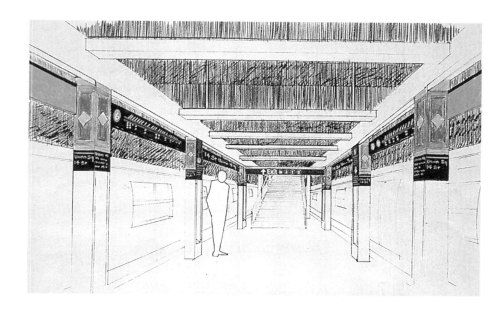

Concept: Subway Signage

A sketch of subway entrance Signage that visually announces and signifies the subway. The passenger is given in-

Figure 8.21 **NY Transit #10.**

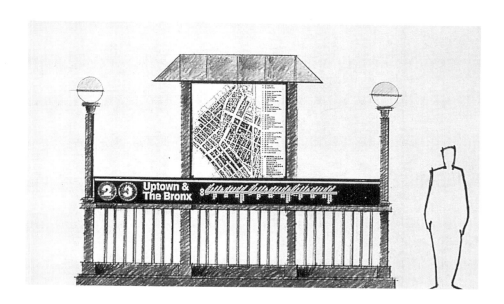

formation on the train before entering the station, the surrounding area is identified, and, if this design was used throughout the system, it would clearly and visually announce the presence of a subway. (*Courtesy of NY Transit.*)

Concept: Integrated Signage System

Siteguide is a comprehensive, interactive, information and directory system for large environments. It combines interactive technology with traditional Signage to allow a user to explore a site by touch screen technology. Using a magazine theme, the graphics designed for the system display up-to-date information and directions about shops, transportation, restaurants, residents, and neighborhood events. Upon selecting a destination, a map appears on the screen with audio and visual directions to the desired destination. A detailed instruction sheet, printed at the kiosk, can also be requested. A phone is provided which can provide instant communication with the destination selection. Restaurant reservations can also be made through the service.

Five basic components make up the family of Siteguide products: an interactive directory, kiosks, Electronic Poster System, Newslights System, and Static Signage. The following illustrations (8.23 to 8.34, inclusive) show products developed for the World Financial Center, in New York City, to blend in with its design. The system provides an array of information, from news to menus to directions. Access to the huge number of areas, products, and services available at the Center is relayed in a clear and comprehensive way when using this public integrated-information system. (See illustrations for more information about the system's components.) (*Courtesy of E.D.I.*)

Concept: Integrated Signage System

Kiosks house the Interactive Directory and Newslights LED displays. (*Courtesy of E.D.I.*)

Figure 8.22 **Siteguide. Designed by Edwin Schlossberg Incorporated for Insightguide, an information systems development and production company.**

Figure 8.23 **Siteguide Kiosks.**

Figure 8.24 **Siteguide Kiosks.**

Concept: Integrated Signage System

Kiosks provide interactive services and voice communication tailored to the individual user. (*Courtesy of E.D.I.*)

Concept: Integrated Signage System

This uses videodisk technology, combining audio-video (AV) and still photography, to present a visual image.

Capabilities of the directory are:

1. AV of an entire environment.

2. AV directions to a destination on the site from the user's location.

3. Printed directions of the easiest route.

4. Alphabetical listing of all places, services, and products on the site.

5. Categorized listing of all places, services, and products on the site.

6. Advertising, menus, and announcement inserts.

7. Special events, performances, and calender inserts.

Figure 8.25 **Siteguide Interactive Directory.**

A monthly report, outlining how the directory was used and which kiosks were used, provides useful programming data. (*Courtesy of E.D.I.*)

Concept: Integrated Signage System

The touch screen provides instant access. (*Courtesy of E.D.I.*)

Figure 8.26 **Siteguide Interactive Directory.**

Concept: Integrated Signage System

A typical restaurant information page. (*Courtesy of E.D.I.*)

Figure 8.27 **Siteguide Interactive Directory.**

Concept: Integrated Signage System
Opening page of restaurant directory with options on the touch screen. (*Courtesy of E.D.I.*)

Figure 8.28 **Siteguide Interactive Directory.**

Concept: Integrated Signage System
Printed instructions are available at each kiosk. (*Courtesy of E.D.I.*)

Figure 8.29 **Siteguide Interactive Directory.**

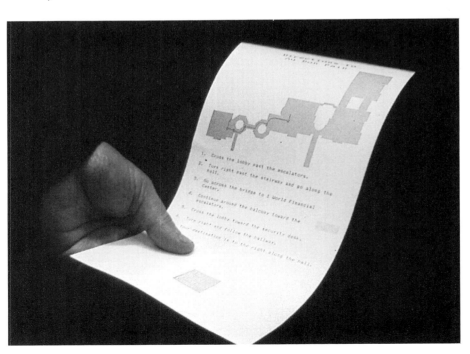

Concept: Integrated Signage System

A series of ceiling-mounted video monitors with computer graphic animation. Messages continuously roll across the screens announcing events, concerts, etc. and capturing attention. (*Courtesy of E.D.I.*)

Concept: Integrated Signage System

Scrolling LED displays situated on kiosks highlight international, business, and financial news, weather, and sports. (*Courtesy of E.D.I.*)

Figure 8.30 Electronic Poster System.

Figure 8.31 Newslights System.

Concept: Integrated Signage System

Static Signage fills in the gaps between electronic technology and way finding devices. It provides visual clues and direction. (*Courtesy of E.D.I.*)

Figure 8.32 Static Signage.

Concept: Integrated Signage System

The medallions based on colors and forms found on the site represent the eight major architectural components and provide keys to way finding. The Winter Garden, the pyramids of the courtyard, the marble patterns, and the building tops are all represented in the medallions. (*Courtesy of E.D.I.*)

Figure 8.33 **Static Signage.**

Concept: Integrated Signage System

Traditional Signage provides way finding, visual comfort, and assurance to the casual browser/walker. It identifies

Figure 8.34 **Static Signage.**

where you are, simply, and directs unambiguously. (*Courtesy of E.D.I.*)

Train Scenario

Subways and trains are becoming more accessible. As access becomes a reality the Signage, space planning, and clarity of egress make traveling a pleasure for everyone. Vignelli Associates, along with consultants and the New York City Transit Authority, developed this train to be a paragon of access. The Signage is clear, precise, and instructive, and is reinforced by voice and sound. (*Courtesy of MTA, New York City Transit.*)

Figure 8.35 **NYCTA Test Train, 1993. Designed by Vignelli Associates.**

Train Scenario

By eliminating the conductor's cabin, found at the end of every car, space was freed to increased accessibility and seating. The cars look bigger, brighter, and are safer because the passenger's view from one car to the next is unobstructed. Simpler grab bars and rails make the cars' interiors less complicated and safer. (*Courtesy of MTA, New York City Transit.*)

Figure 8.36 **NYCTA Test Train, 1993. Designed by Vignelli Associates.**

Train Scenario

The arrangement of seating and grab bars creates a smooth, even flow through the cars. (*Courtesy MTA, New York City Transit.*)

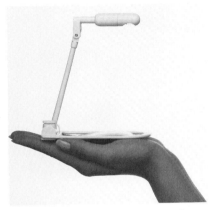

Figure 8.37 **NYCTA Test Train, 1993. Designed by Vignelli Associates.**

Figure 8.38 **Itty Bitty Book Light by Zelco Industries.**

Figure 8.39 **Thumper Traveler by Zelco Industries.**

Figure 8.40 **Magnificent Magnifying Mirror by Zelco Industries.**

Product: Book Light

Easily packed for travel the book light clips onto the back of a book to illuminate reading with cool, brilliant light, to focus light where it's needed. (*Courtesy of Zelco.*)

Product: Travel Alarm Clock

An easy-to-operate alarm clock that features a large thumper pad that turns off the alarm, sets a four-minute snooze control, and backlights the numbers for easy viewing in the dark. It also features large, easy-to-read controls. (*Courtesy of Zelco.*)

Product: Magnifying Mirror

This mirror is lightweight and provides 3× magnification. It runs on either AC or its own self-contained rechargeable battery, so it's portable. The replaceable bulbs provide soft, glare-free illumination. (*Courtesy of Zelco.*)

Product: Personal Light

The red light beam allows the pupils to remain open for the best legibility in dim light. Small type is magnified five times. Ideal for reading maps, menus, and theater programs. (*Courtesy of Zelco.*)

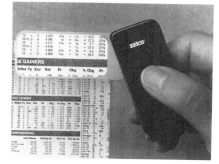

Figure 8.41 **The Skinny Little Lumifer by Zelco Industries.**

RANDOM THOUGHTS ON UNIVERSAL DESIGN

Most people see to photograph, I photograph to see.

The reason a photograph is easier to see than the scene it represents is simple to understand. A photograph is not reality, but an abstraction of reality. Even the most correctly developed photograph is a high-contrast abstraction of the object it represents. Thousands of colors, shades, hues, and textures are reduced to a few shades of gray between black and white. Confusing shapes and distances are reduced to a two-dimensional representation. In this world, millions of Americans can see what would otherwise be a blurr.

George Covington

Product: Camera

One of the smallest, thinnest, and easy to use of the "Point and Shoot" cameras, the T4 can focus to 14" and uses a variety of flash modes for control.

The design of this camera demands almost no eyesight to use. By pressing the shutter button half way down, a green Light Emitting Diode (LED) outside and to the right of the viewfinder tells you when the image is in focus. A red LED below the green LED tells when the flash is needed and ready. (*Courtesy of Yaschica Optical Division, Kyocera Electronics, Inc.*)

Figure 8.42 **Yashica 35MM T4 Camera with Carl Zeiss Tessar T Lens.**

Product: Camera

This camera is the smallest and easiest to use of the disposable flash 35MM class. Its light weight and simplicity of use make it accessible to most people. (*Courtesy of Eastman Kodak Company.*)

Figure 8.43 **Kodak Funsaver Pocket Camera.**

Figure 8.44 **The Camera Cap—Products for the Global Thrill Seeker. Designed by Erin Hoover as a thesis while at Pratt Institute.**

Concept: The Global Thrill Seeker

This is a cap that takes pictures as programmed on the touch screen or hands-free, per verbal instructions via a built-in microphone. (It also floats.) Erin Hoover states, "With the miniaturization of high-tech gadgets, we are rapidly evolving into walking telecommunications devices—*Homowirelessus*. So I ask, why not exchange portability for wear ability." (*Courtesy of Pratt Institute and Erin Hoover.*)

Concept: The Global Thrill Seeker

This Global Positioning System is a tracking device which allows one to locate the wearer. This function is enhanced by the Satellite Shoes' ability to also receive global positioning information (see Figure 8.46). (*Courtesy of Pratt Institute and Erin Hoover.*)

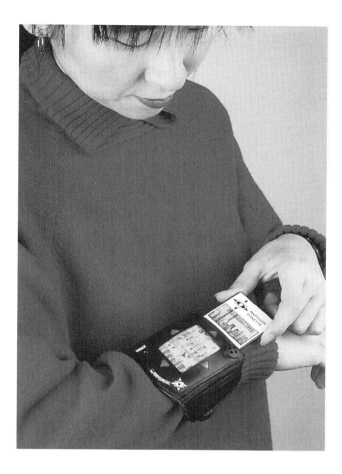

Figure 8.45 **The Wrist Guide—Products for the Global Thrill Seeker. Designed by Erin Hoover as a thesis while at Pratt Institute.**

Concept: The Global Thrill Seeker

The shoes provide real-time feedback as the wearer moves toward his or her destination. They also have a toe-mounted light. (*Courtesy of Pratt Institute and Erin Hoover.*)

Figure 8.46 **Satellite Shoes— Products for the Global Thrill Seeker. Designed by Erin Hoover as a thesis while at Pratt Institute.**

Figure 8.47 **Data Scarf—Products for the Global Thrill Seeker. Designed by Erin Hoover as a thesis while at Pratt Institute.**

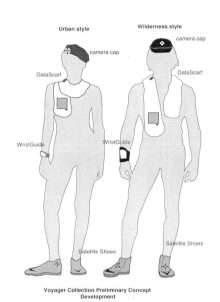

Figure 8.48 **Voyager Collection—Products for the Global Thrill Seeker. Designed by Erin Hoover as a thesis while at Pratt Institute.**

Figure 8.49 **Ticker Shopping. Designed by Marcus Hohl at the Royal College of Art in London for** *Design Age* **Competition sponsored by RSA.**

Concept: The Global Thrill Seeker

This is a wearable computer that links all the other wearable equipment in the Global Thrill Seeker Series (and also dispenses insect repellent or perfume). (*Courtesy of Pratt Institute and Erin Hoover.*)

Concept: The Global Thrill Seeker

The fully dressed Global Thrill Seeker. (*Courtesy of Pratt Institute and Erin Hoover.*)

Concept: Handheld Scanner

A handheld scanner for supermarket shopping designed to give the user the choice of "ticking" items off the shelf. The store would be arranged on two floors: One floor would have display shelves; on the other there would be a stockroom where orders would be filled. The "Ticker" is ring shaped and worn on the wrist. It is used to scan bar codes and place an order for those items scanned. Checkout is easy, with the packed orders delivered directly to the person's home or car. (*Courtesy of Marcus Hohl,* Design Age, *Royal College of Art, U.K.*)

Concept: Escalator

A vertical transport system for everyone. The design of the escalator uses platforms, instead of steps, traveling in the line of the escalator, combining lift technology and escalator technology to provide a constant barrier-free system. This system combines the security of an elevator with the efficiency of an escalator. (*Courtesy of Michael Kenneth Drain Design Age, Royal College of Art, U.K.*)

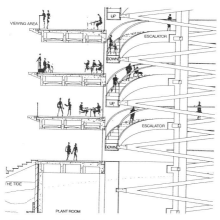

Figure 8.50 Platform Escalator. Designed by Michael Kenneth Drain at the Royal College of Art in London for *Design Age* Competition sponsored by RSA.

Concept: Automated Teller Machine (ATM)

The design intends to improve the accessibility for everyone. By designing the lowest shelf height at 35 inches it is possible for both sitting and standing people to use the ATM. All points of interaction have braille and illuminate. The screen tilts. The ATM card is inserted only partially to permit easy retrieval. The cash dispenser has a large surface area and deposits are made into a drawer which is easier to see and feel. The keypad buttons are large and isolated making use very easy and very safe. (*Courtesy of Julie Troka, student at the Center for Creative Studies, Detroit, and AT&T.*)

Figure 8.51 AT&T Self-Service Product for the Disabled. An Automated Teller Machine (ATM) designed by Julie Troka of Ohio State University, working as a 1993 summer intern at the AT&T Design Center.

Figure 8.52 **IDEO Urban Bus.**

Concept: Transit Scenario

The Design Business Association (DBA), in association with Apple Computer, sponsored an event where design consultancies could demonstrate their design process through the presentation of a conceptual design. IDEO's presentation, directed by Oliver Bayley, focused on three different people using different aspects of the transit system. (*Courtesy of IDEO Product Development.*)

> **RANDOM THOUGHTS ON UNIVERSAL DESIGN**
>
> "Universal Design transcends the divisions of gender, age, fashion, and location and communicates purpose to the beholder while simultaneously appealing to their individual aesthetic need."
>
> *Oliver Bayley*

Using scenarios to illustrate design and to generate "user models" helps create ideas by putting designers in "someone else's shoes." IDEO used scenarios to project into the future of urban transportation. The year is 1998, the city is London, UK, the people are Agnes, a 77-year-old widower, Sarah and her two children, Alison and Ann, and Sam, a foreign traveler. The concepts were developed around these people trying to anticipate their needs and where these needs might occur.

Character Profile

Name : Agnes
Age : 73 yrs
Status : Widow living alone

• Weather protection

• Easy board buses

• Smooth motion buses

• Instant / readable information displays

Figure 8.53 **IDEO Urban Bus Agnes Profile.**

Concept: Transit Scenario (Agnes)

We join Agnes at the bus stop. She used to dread the journey across town to visit her sister, but now enjoys the new buses and those enclosed shelters which offer protection from the weather and a place to sit. Agnes has registered her bus card at the service point machine, and keeps an eye on the arrival display. (*Courtesy of IDEO Product Development.*)

Concept: Transit Scenario (Agnes)

The display and the speakers announce the bus's arrival and confirms its route as it draws to a stop outside the shelter doors, which open for Agnes to walk onto the bus at the same level. It is much easier to walk up the bus shelter ramp at her own pace rather than being hurried to negotiate a high step when the bus arrives. (*Courtesy of IDEO Product Development.*)

Figure 8.54 **IDEO Urban Bus.**

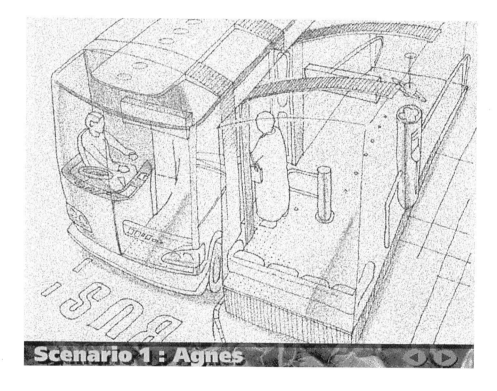

Scenario 1 : Agnes

Concept: Transit Scenario (Sarah)

Sarah and her two girls, Alison and Ann, use the bus to go to Sainsburys. It is a bit further than the local shops, but the bus journey is a pleasant outing. (*Courtesy of IDEO Product Development.*)

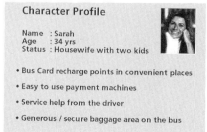

Character Profile

Name : Sarah
Age : 34 yrs
Status : Housewife with two kids

• Bus Card recharge points in convenient places
• Easy to use payment machines
• Service help from the driver
• Generous / secure baggage area on the bus

Figure 8.55 **IDEO Urban Bus Sarah Profile.**

Concept: Transit Scenario (Sarah)

Sarah likes the new easy-to-understand machines, or "service points" as they are now called. Her bus card has

Figure 8.56 **IDEO Urban Bus.**

nearly expired, as she can see from the "thermometer" gauge on it, and it needs recharging to get them home. The service point in the supermarket arcade offers a convenient place for them to do this. (*Courtesy of IDEO Product Development.*)

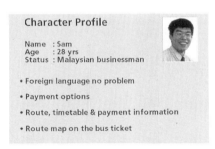

Character Profile

Name : Sam
Age : 28 yrs
Status : Malaysian businessman

• Foreign language no problem
• Payment options
• Route, timetable & payment information
• Route map on the bus ticket

Figure 8.57 **IDEO Urban Bus Sam Profile.**

Concept: Transit Scenario (Sam)

Foreign travelers are an important user group. This is Sam's first trip to London from his native Malaysia. He is intrigued to try the London bus system, which is certainly different from the one at home. He is, however, not clear where the buses go to and how much they cost. (*Courtesy of IDEO Product Development.*)

Concept: Transit Scenario (Sam)

Sam arrives at the bus stop, which he notices has some kind of electronic vending machine incorporated into the structure. Beside it is the list of buses available, and the places they stop at. Sam examines the list and finds the museum

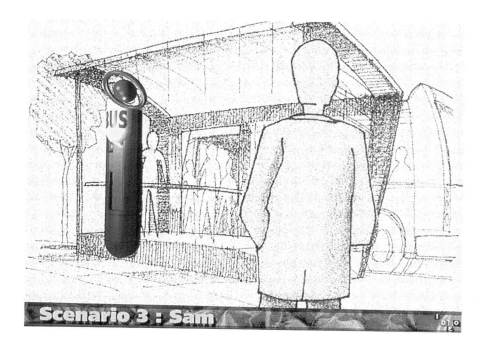

Figure 8.58 **IDEO Urban Bus.**

he is going to, so he knows which bus to take, and the cost. (*Courtesy of IDEO Product Development.*)

Concept: Transit Scenario Checklist

Working on this project IDEO developed a checklist of desirable features that seems appropriate for any urban form of transport:

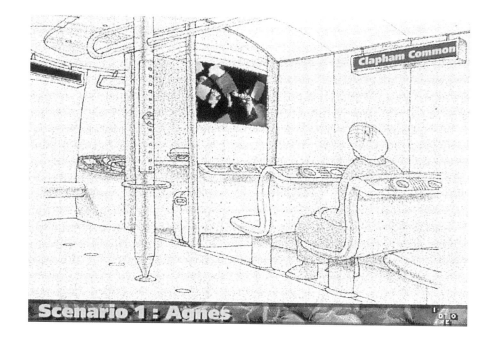

Figure 8.59 **IDEO Urban Bus.**

1. Design that considers children and older people.

2. Designs that cater for disability factors like mobility, speech, sight, and hearing impairments.

3. Designs appropriate for multicultural users.

4. More helpful information and easier interactions.

5. Bringing the driver back into prominence in the service of passengers, as the system is more humanized.

6. A service approach to ticket machine design.

7. Improved lighting for buses and shelters for a more welcoming environment.

8. All this leading to a more functional, attractive, and comfortable bus. (*Courtesy of IDEO Product Development.*)

TRAVEL TRANSITIONS TO REMEMBER

Transitions from one space, service, or product to another often present barriers whether physical or psychological.

1. Threshold Access: Entrance; Doors

2. Vertical Assent: Stairs; Elevator; Escalator

3. Train Access: Station; Ticket Purchase; Seats; Restroom

4. Bus Access: Bus Stop; Maps; Wheelchair Accessibility

5. Car Access

6. Airlines and Airplane Access: Airport; Ticket and Baggage Processing; Seating; Restroom

7. Boat-Ship Access: Docks; Ramps; Rooms; Bathrooms; Recreation

8. Hotel Access: Lobby; Staircases or Elevators; Rooms; Bathroom

9. Restroom Access: Doorways; Fixtures; Facilities

10. Technological Access: Communications; Computers

11. Store Access

12. Communication Access

13. Outdoor Access: Play Areas; Fields

☑ CHECK LIST
Accessible Travel

1. Design products for dual voltage.

2. Controls on vending devices should be unambiguous, simple, and intuitive. The keypad entry at ATMs, ticket-token vending machines, and telephones should be accessible to everyone. Are there braille indicators?

3. Credit card, telephone card, and transit card use should be clear and unambiguous. Are there braille indicators? Are the instructions both visual and verbal? Can graphic symbols explain the process better?

4. Everyone doesn't speak the same language—is Signage easily understood, using visual, tactile, braille, and International Symbols?

5. Warning tracks warn everyone. Contrasting colors, and changes in resiliency and texture on walking surfaces alert everyone to dangerous situations.

6. Use Universal Symbols to direct and inform.

7. Use contrasting, nonglare colors on all stairway risers and doorways, and to announce changes in direction or level.

8. Illuminate stairwells. Are handrails clearly defined, painted in a high-contrast color to the wall? Are they continuous with breaks at exit points? Do the stair edges contrast with the color of the tread? Mark edges of stairs, ramps, platforms, and rails by changing texture or using a high-contrast color.

9. Use every sense (i.e., sight, sound, touch, even smell) to direct and guide. Don't forget to use layout maps showing where the person is in relation to a desired destination, such as a subway or cruise ship "map."

10. Stations and stops should be announced clearly and well in advance, to allow riders with limited mobility to prepare for exit.

11. Communication devices should be available not only physically but also in as many forms as possible. Telephones should provide both audio and text.

12. Written instructions should be concise, simple, and available on an audio-visual display.

13. All insertion points for keys, cards, money, tokens, etc. should be tapered and self-aligning to guide the user during insertion.

14. Controls such as handles, locks, outlets, switches, faucets, and thermostats should be reachable by all. Outlets and faucets should provide protection from shock or scalding.

15. Safety devices such as peepholes, fire extinguishers, fire alarms, and smoke detectors should be accessible to everyone. Are both audio and visual signals available?

16. Are restrooms and their facilities accessible to all people? Do they accommodate wheelchairs?

17. Cameras, videocams, and audiocassette recorders should be easy to use.

18. Color and texture-code everything.

CHAPTER 9

THE TOOLS AND COMPUTERS

"As I write this one letter at a time," says George Covington, "I am eating words once spoken in vain about these infernal machines."

A computer is a window on the world, with E-mail or any other communication means once you have the modem, everything and everywhere is available—from your bank statement, which is so easy to balance with the new software, to walks through museums. Computers will change your life.

Computers are becoming how we talk and especially how we communicate with each other. Once you open the window, a virtual storm will blow in. Whether you like it or not, pun intended, the medium is the message. Like all metaphors, a sudden and clear reality will encompass whatever romantic notion was embodied. As voice input technology becomes available we will be talking to ourselves or, if we like to, the machines. Although voice technology is a proven thing, an office or household full of people talking to machines is unlikely in the near future, so we must remain with the standard "QWERTY" keyboard.

Figure 9.1 **238 Microsoft Natural Computer Keyboard.** *(Photo: Michael Jones.)*

Feature: Natural Keyboard

The Natural Keyboard design developed by Ziba Design for Microsoft Corporation. It offers an integrated palm pad located at the base of the keyboard to improve shoulder and back comfort by providing a natural resting place during breaks. The surface of the keyboard is gently raised at the center to further enhance user comfort. The design helps prevent fatigue and carpal tunnel syndrome, frequently associated with typing. Microsoft did something about the way we type information into the machines by developing the Natural Keyboard in conjunction with Ziba Design. With 40 million people using keyboards a natural one that helps alleviate some of the problems like carpal tunnel syndrome and fatigue associated with typing is a welcome advance. Ziba Design conducted eight months of extensive research into keyboard ergonomics, user preferences, and anthropometric standards. Ziba collaborated with ergonomic experts nationwide with the goal of mainstreaming ergonomics, making them available to a variety of computer users.

The Natural Keyboard is designed to alleviate the wrist deviation and forearm pronation that can lead to repetitive stress injuries and caters to a variety of postures and typing styles without the need for **special** adjustments. "Special" is the key word in the idea; eliminating **special** from the design vocabulary is a major goal of Universal Design.

> ### 💡 RANDOM THOUGHTS ON UNIVERSAL DESIGN
>
> My general intent for these designs was to assist physically challenged individuals with everyday tasks, but these solutions not only help the physically challenged, but also assist the temporarily disabled.
>
> *Pedro M. Alfonso*

Product: Hardware

Controls that can be inadvertently either turned on or off present hazards. Pedro M. Alfonso's goal in the redesign of this reset control was first, to prevent inadvertent use and second, to enhance the ability of everyone to locate and activate the control. Figure shows the existing condition Pedro started with. Even though the button is large, bright in color, and has a shape reserved to itself within the boundaries, users accidentally tripped it, at times causing loss of data. (*Courtesy of International Business Machine Corporation.*)

Figure 9.2 **IBM RISC System/ 6000 Reset Control. Designed by Pedro M. Alfonso.**

Product: Hardware

Addressing the problem of accidental tripping, the obvious solution was to reduce the size of the button and recess it into the mounting bezel. This solution, the first to go into production, made it almost impossible to inadvertently activate the switch. "Normal" users are required to use a pencillike object to activate. The ridge frame around the opening assists the visually impaired users in locating the switch area. (*Courtesy of International Business Machine Corporation.*)

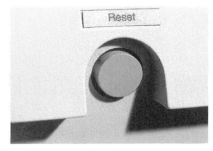

Figure 9.3 **IBM RISC System/ 6000 Reset Control. Designed by Pedro M. Alfonso.**

Product: Hardware

The second iteration offers a larger target area, an elongated circle with a sculpted recess that directs the user to the button. Small details are more important than big pictures if they are the controlling kind. (*Courtesy of International Business Machine Corporation.*)

Figure 9.4 **IBM RISC System/ 6000 Reset Control. Designed by Pedro M. Alfonso.**

Product: Hardware

This machine delivers the functions of four machines in one compact desktop unit. It faxes, copies, prints, and scans. (*Courtesy of Mita AF-1000.*)

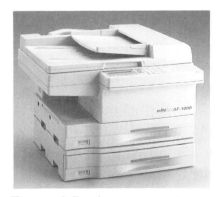

Figure 9.5 **Mita AF-1000 Integrated Imaging System.**

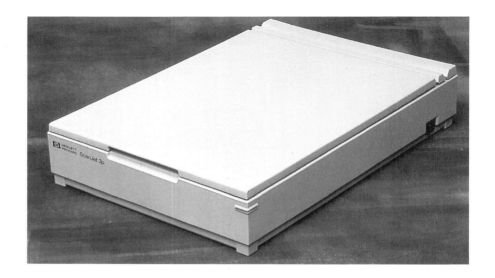

Figure 9.6 **Hewlett Packard ScanJet 3p Scanner.**

Product: Hardware

The HP ScanJet 3p Scanner comes with text recognition and automatic image-scanning software that enhances document images. It also has a copy utility when used with the scanner. Integrated scanning software allows the user to complete most scanning functions with a single click. (*Courtesy of Hewlett Packard.*)

Products: Hardware/Software

Using the latest technology Arkenstone creates tools that overcome barriers to information. An Open Book is a com-

Figure 9.7 & 9.8 **Arkenstone's An Open Book.**

RANDOM THOUGHTS ON UNIVERSAL DESIGN

Will we be talking to ourselves or machines? Voice recognition software and hardware are realities. You don't have to be rich to talk to yourself anymore. Voice-activated "stuff" is here and it is going to make access immediate and uncomplicated. The "Open Book" hardware/software of Arkenstone makes it possible to listen to what we might have read.

Bruce Hannah

plete reading machine that scans printed material, then automatically "reads" it aloud. An Open Book has the capability to hold thousands of pages in its library. It consists of a scanner which "sees" the page, the Reading Machine which records, translates, and saves the scanned words into text, a keypad for control of the operation, and a voice synthesizer which reads the page back to you. (*Courtesy of Arkenstone.*)

Product: Hardware

This paper-port plugs into a Macintosh printer or modem port. When a printed page is inserted, the Paperport scans it, automatically activates its own software, and displays the scanned material on screen. Electronic copies, to be filed, edited, annotated, and/or printed, are also produced. (*Courtesy of Visioneer.*)

Figure 9.9 **Paperport by Visioneer.**

Product: Hardware

This Powerbook has the power capacity of a Quadra, but is portable and lightweight (seven pounds). It features a built-in trackpad, long-life batteries (with a solar recharger), and

Figure 9.10 **Apple Powerbook 5300. *(Photo: John Greenleigh)***

a full range of colors in its memory. (*Courtesy of Apple Computer, Inc.*)

Figure 9.11 **Apple Macintosh Performa 636CD.** *(Photo: John Greenleigh)*

Product: Hardware

The Performa aids the user in a myriad of everyday tasks, such as sending a fax, exploring the Internet, making phone calls, balancing a checkbook, spell checking a document without using a dictionary, playing games, creating a calendar, and keeping an address "book" up to date.

It also provides the user, despite his or her skills, the capability of designing personalized greeting cards, enlarging and retouching photographs, and even engineering a boat.

The personal computer lowers (or eliminates) restrictions and increases (and enhances) accessibility. (*Courtesy of Apple Computer, Inc.*)

Product: Hardware

The built-in recognition software transforms on-screen handwriting (using a stylus) into on-screen text which can be printed out, making typing unnecessary. (Neatness does help, however, as Newton still has trouble deciphering some handwriting.)

The user can also use the stylus to draw or to enter information with the on-screen keyboard or text and icons. There is also a built-in calendar and address "book." With an optional modem, the user can send and receive faxes and E-mail, access on-line services, and "network" with other Newtons. It prints formatted text as well as a screen "dump," which is an exact printout of what is on the screen. A truly amazing little computer, that despite its short comings in the handwritten-recognition department, goes along way to accessing and organizing information for just about anyone anywhere. (*Courtesy of Apple Computer, Inc.*)

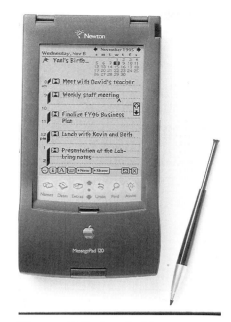

Figure 9.12 **Apple Newton Message Pad 120 personal digital assistant (PDA).** *(Photo: John Greenleigh)*

Product: Hardware

The most startling feature of the 701 is the full-sized keyboard, which moves into position when the ThinkPad is opened. The full-size TrackWrite expanding keyboard emerges from the machine, which turns on automatically as the keyboard emerges. With the full-sized keyboard and full-sized screen this small computer functions like a full-sized one. The elegantly simple mechanism that drives the keyboard owes its life to John Kardis's playful nature and his child's classic wooden blocks. While playing blocks with his child, John realized that the triangular blocks slipped by each other and could reform into a rectangle from a square by slipping by each other. This led to the TrackWrite keyboard design.

The ThinkPad screen folds 180 degrees so that it slips under a large monitor and eliminates the need to detach and reattach the screen in order to dock. Sam Lucente's design group work with what they call "user maps" to develop profiles of end-user needs. This is an approach that helps define and guide designers when developing a product. The full-sized keyboard came out of one of these user-map sessions when the profile that was developed indicated a need for the clarity and ease of data entry provided only by a full-sized keyboard. The integration of hardware and software

Figure 9.13 **IBM ThinkPad 701, a.k.a. Butterfly. Invented by John Kardis, designed by Sam Lucente, Program Manager, Strategic Design and Robert Tennant, Advisory Industrial Designer, both of IBM, and Richard Sapper, IBM Industrial Design Consultant.**

in the ThinkPad is also obvious in the simple battery maintenance and save features. Features like a speaker phone, answering machine, and fax machine are already built in, along with an infrared wireless file transfer which eliminates plugs when transferring data from one ThinkPad notebook to another, or to other infrared-compatible machines.

Universal Design? We think the accessibility built into this machine is moving it closer to universality than most. (*Courtesy of International Business Machines Corporation.*)

The Universally Designed Work Space

The concept of the Universally Designed Workstation is simple to understand. By selecting and combining certain electronic equipment and office fixtures, a work space is created for maximum use by individuals with disabilities. Slight modifications made in a work space accommodates different types and degrees of disability.

The following work space is for a legally blind individual who has less than five percent usable vision.

EQUIPMENT

1. Power Mac 6100, 12 meg RAM

   Internal fax/modem

   250 meg internal hard drive

   3X CD-ROM

   High-resolution monitor

Extended keyboard

Trackball

2. Apple Personal Laser 320

3. Hewlett Packard ScanJet 11cx

Caere Omni Page Pro (OCR software)

COMPUTER TRANSITIONS
TO REMEMBER

Transitions from one space, service, or product to another often present barriers whether physical or psychological.

1. Keyboard Access

2. Printer Access

3. CPU Access

4. Mouse Access

5. On/Off Switch Access

6. Software Access

7. Customer Service Access

8. Ordering Access

9. Screen Access

10. Supplies Access

11. Scanner Access

✓ CHECK LIST
Accessible Home Computers

1. Letters and numbers on keyboards should be 24-point type.

2. The size of letters on the screen can make a difference in the user's ability to read, use the best type size and font for the degree of low vision.

3. Dark-on-light lettering is easier to read and adjust. Adjusting the contrast can make a big difference in the ability to read text. Color and size of the lettering on a screen can affect the ability to read comfortably.

4. Proper lighting is important. (A user should avoid sudden changes in light level and take frequent rest periods to rest their eyes. Looking at infinity can help eyes rest, by focusing on nothing.)

5. Eliminate glare on screens. Using polarizing filters over CRTs and VDTs can help eliminate glare.

6. Avoid positioning computers near windows because of the glare from them. Turn monitors 90 degrees from windows or provide blinds over the windows or antiglare for monitors.

7. Keep VDTs and CRTs 20 inches from eyes.

8. Use palm and wrist rests.

9. Use a footrest to relieve back and leg strain.

10. Use adjustable keyboards and monitor supports, which have horizontal, vertical, and lateral adjustments. Use ergonomically designed keyboards.

11. Use a copy stand so that eyes move only vertically or horizontally. Horizontal movement is less tiring.

12. Use monitor lifts to bring the monitor into the right focal area for the user.

13. Are controls accessible but designed to prevent unintended use?

14. Can books and data be "read" aloud by the equipment for the hearing impaired?

CHAPTER 10

THE PARK AND RECREATION

Sunday in the park continues to be a universal experience, whether it includes playing, picnicking, fishing, or just people watching. Access to the park and its surroundings takes on more meaning when more activities are available to everyone. Children with disabilities who interact with able-bodied children are more likely to expect other areas of society to be equally accessible to them as they grow older. If children do not face barriers created by others they will not accept barriers as adults. Access to recreation and play constitute a vital part of everyone's life. Play is an important activity that builds strength, coordination, social skills, and self confidence. Quality outdoor play experiences often contribute to improved performance and attitude in the classroom as well. Disabled parents are able to enjoy the experience of play with their able-bodied children. Playing with Grandma and Grandpa at the park can be fun and rewarding for both child and adult. Making playgrounds accessible allows interaction to occur. Play structures that restrict interactive play, by either physical or psychological barriers, make some of us spectators. Watching can be fun but participation promotes learning. Grandma wants to play as much as anyone—why shouldn't she?

Concept: Play Equipment

This modular play structure was created using a challenge-levels system that rates play components by their difficulty of use. Building a particular play unit out of roughly equal numbers of components from each of three challenge levels, ensures that children of all abilities will be able to play together. The Scramble Climber entrance (lower right) allows children with mobility impairments to enter the equipment. Shock-

Figure 10.1 **Explorers Modular Play Equipment System from PlayDesigns.**

absorbing ground covers, like the rubber material shown here, support wheeled access. (*Courtesy of PlayDesigns.*)

Figure 10.2 **Modular Play Equipment System Detail. Tiered platforms from PlayDesigns and Playworld Systems.**

Concept: Play Equipment

This simple detail of low, wide steps allows children to run, walk, scramble, and crawl to new heights. The feature makes climbing easier for everyone and possible for children who may have only crawling-locomotion abilities. (*Courtesy of PlayDesigns.*)

Concept: Play Equipment

Playscenes shifts the focus of play activity away from the physical strength approach of traditional play equipment. Instead, the Gas Station makes imagination, social interaction, and role playing the focus of play. It is one of a series of 3-D sketches of sites of daily human activity and drama, along with The Diner, The Drive Thru, The Theater, and The Sailboat. By presenting ground-based events, Playscenes allows all people to participate without "announcing" their ability. (*Courtesy of PlayDesigns.*)

Figure 10.3 **Playscenes from PlayDesigns: The Gas Station. (Winner of a Gold Industrial Design Excellence Award IDEA, presented by *Business Week* and the Industrial Design Society of America, 1995.)**

"A playground system must ensure that every child, regardless of ability, will find activities he or she can use, while encouraging disabled and able-bodied children to interact and learn from one another."

Kevin Owens
Director of Innovations
PlayDesigns and Playworld Systems

Concept: Play Equipment

The Drive Thru presents a fun, role-playing imaginative activity for children with all sorts of locomotive abilities. (*Courtesy of PlayDesigns.*)

Figure 10.4 **Playscenes from PlayDesigns. The Drive Thru. (Winner of a Gold Industrial Design Excellence Award IDEA presented by** *Business Week* **and the Industrial Design Society of America, 1995.)**

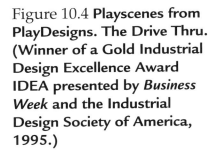

Figure 10.5 **U-Bounce Modular Play Component from Playworld Systems.**

Concept: Play Equipment

This component brings a new bouncing activity to the school or park playground. Its handholds and rubber platform allow it to be used by children of all heights, seated or standing. Its simple action is easily activated by children of a wide range of strengths and abilities, to develop balance and gross motor skills. Its motion is proportional to the

"While making playground structures accessible impacts the recreation budget, most costs are less than anticipated. In addition, it is being discovered that accessible components make the play environment easier for all children to use, not just the physically disabled."

Kevin Owens
Director of Innovations
PlayDesigns and Playworld Systems

Figure 10.6 **First Play Soft Modular Play Equipment for Toddlers from PlayDesigns. (Gold Industrial Design Excellence Award IDEA, from *Business Week* and the Industrial Design Society Of America, 1993.)**

weight of the user—the smaller the child, the less challenging its action.(*Courtesy of PlayWorld.*)

Concept: Toddler Play Equipment

This design was the first commercial play system to exhibit full Universal Design. Low, soft climbing surfaces encourage gross motor skill development, and the bright fabric activity panels teach basic fine motor and cognitive skills, such as hand-eye coordination and shape recognition. (*Courtesy of PlayDesigns.*)

"A designed object, product, building, or landscape earns the term 'Universal Design' only if, in its final built state, it works properly—in one form—for everyone."

Kevin Owens
Director of Innovations
PlayDesigns and Playworld Systems

Figure 10.7 **First Play from PlayDesigns, detail. (*Courtesy of PlayDesigns.*)**

Figure 10.8 **First Play from PlayDesigns, detail. (Gold Industrial Design Excellence Award IDEA from** *Business Week* **and the Industrial Design Society Of America, 1993.)**

Concept: Toddler Play Equipment

First Play activities also address auditory senses as shown here in the "Chimes Activity Panel." Gold Industrial Design Excellence Award IDEA, from *Business Week* and the Industrial Design Society Of America, 1993.

Concept: Toddler Play Equipment

Low, soft decks and padded handholds make mobility through the equipment easier for all children at an age when they are first learning to walk, climb, and explore the world. These features also make it possible for the same equipment to serve the needs of children with disabilities by providing a soft, friendly environment to practice gross motor skills. (*Courtesy of PlayDesigns.*)

Concept: Universal Design for Ease of Assembly

Some assembly required. Dreaded words to anyone who has ever tried to follow instructions. And who even tries to follow the instructions? Usually they are stuck in the bottom of the box and are indecipherable once you find them, anyway. Universal Design should include in its priorities the concept of easy assembly. Although this seems like a common sense approach, few designers seem to use this scenario when designing products.

Figure 10.9 (right) **Concept drawing: Gladys picks out the parts.**

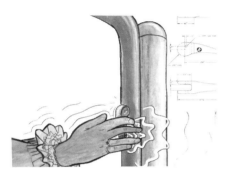

Figure 10.10 **Concept drawing: Gladys installs a cam-lock fastener.**

Kevin Owens, Director of Innovations for Playworld Systems and PlayDesigns believes so strongly in this idea that he has developed products with Universal Design integrated into their assembly in two ways. First, he designed the First Play product line based on a fictional character assembling the equipment with ease, and second, he teamed up with graphic designer, Colleen Shannon of Secret Studio, to develop an assembly manual that features cartoons, minimal text, and humor to present an assembly "comic book."

Figure 10.11 **Concept drawing: Gladys snaps a deck in place.**

Figure 10.12 **Concept drawing: Gladys attached as wall panel.**

"In early product concept drawings we used a scale figure affectionately named "Gladys" as a constant reminder that in child care centers, products are frequently assembled by a single child care worker who may not be particularly strong or familiar with the use of tools or constructions methods," explains Kevin. If Universal Design is considered from the beginning of a project it is possible to include it in all aspects of the use of a product.

Figure 10.13 **Concept drawing: Gladys proudly displays her work.**

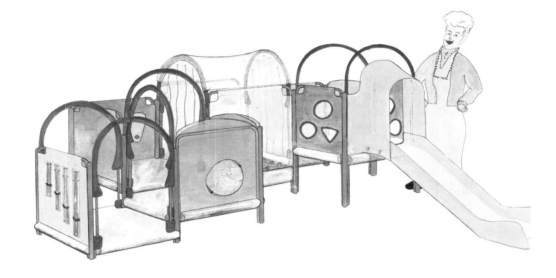

Ultimately, however, the product and its associated manuals must reach the consumer and be fully useable during assembly. Colleen Shannon of Secret Studio explains, "My goal was to dispel the fear of assembly that is so common with products of any size or complexity." Clear, concise, colored images with a touch of humor and very little text make people actually want to "read" the instrument. They also make international installations easier by eliminating the costs and inaccuracies of translation because, in fact, crossing a language border can generate all kinds of "disabilities." Universal Design can vastly improve assembly manuals if this example is any indication. The First Play product line has had only two customer service calls about assembly since its introduction in 1993—a number unheard of in typical commercial play equipment products.

Figure 10.14 **Typical page from First Play Installation Book.** *(Courtesy of Colleen Shannon.)*

Figure 10.15 **Last page from First Play Installation Comic Book. Step 8, frame 11, "time to relax in your new play equipment."** *(Courtesy of Colleen Shannon.)*

Memorial Scenario

The Mall In Washington, DC, is America's park and also a place of tribute. In the nineteenth century monuments were conceived as pilgrimage sites with grand staircases dominat-

Figure 10.16 **Orble designed by Andrew Schloss.**

lattice of fins, and the Orble Flinger, which consists of just fins. With the grip-enhancement quality of fins, anybody can catch and hold the Orble balls. (*Courtesy of Andrew Schloss.*)

Memorial Scenario

The Mall In Washington, DC, is America's park and also a place of tribute. In the nineteenth century monuments were conceived as pilgrimage sites with grand staircases dominating the design, making it possible for only those who can

Figure 10.17 **Korean War Memorial Mural. Designed by Louis Nelson.**

climb to appreciate the sites. The Vietnam War Memorial changed how we think about monuments. The Korean War Monument was planned and designed with access in mind. Its ground-level design allows access to all. Getting close was the whole idea. Louis Nelson's Korean War Memorial Mural Wall, in his words, is "a memorial portrait etched on the nation's heart—a **touchstone** to history," makes the memorial accessible as faces emerge through reflections of sky and trees in the polished granite. Touching the wall is permitted and encouraged. (*Courtesy of Louis Nelson.*)

Product: Crafter's Clamp

Designed to gently hold objects temporarily for assembly. The clamp mimics the hand in size of opening and action. When the handles are squeezed together the jaws open and kinetic energy is stored in the concentric bands. When the handles are released the jaws firmly clamp onto the selected object. The KUDO Clamp does not depend on fine motor skills so it is accessible to a wide audience. (*Courtesy of Steve Visser.*)

Figure 10.18 **KUDO Crafters Clamp. Designed by Steve Visser and Kyle Bennet.** (*Photo by John Underwood.*)

Concepts: Reflective Fountain

The assignment, from Professor Abir Mullick, was "to design a fountain that is universally accessible—a fountain anyone

Figure 10.19 **Tidal Fountain. (The name comes from the shape of a breaking wave.) Designed by Michael Osadciw, Mathew Guthrie, and Michael LaMonica, while design students at the State University of New York at Buffalo.**

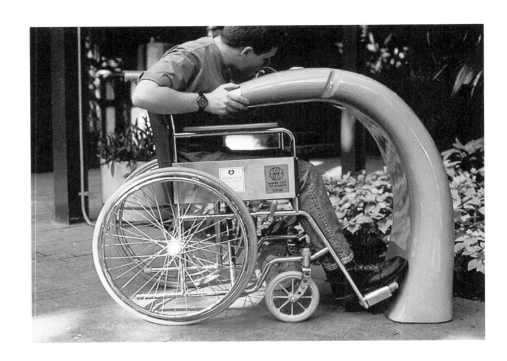

could use." The students' solution allows access without compromising design. (*Courtesy of SUNY/Buffalo Students.*)

💡 *RANDOM THOUGHTS ON UNIVERSAL DESIGN*

"Universal Design is neither a skill nor a content area. It is a goal-oriented approach that aims at addressing the general needs of all users, including unique needs of special users."

Abir Mullick
Associate Professor of Design
SUNY Buffalo

RECREATION TRANSITIONS TO REMEMBER

Transitions from one space, service, or product to another often present barriers whether physical or psychological. At play children need transitions from one activity to another, emphasized by changes in texture, and color that define boundaries.

1. Playground Access: Entranceway; Equipment; Accessible Routes

2. Restroom Access: Doorways; Fixtures; Facilities

3. Food Stand Access

4. Locker Access

5. Seating Access

6. Lighting Access

7. Shelter Access

CHECK LIST
Accessible Play—Universal Design on the Playground

1. Provide an accessible route to and through the playground. Where the accessible route comes within the use of zone play equipment, the route should be paved with a shock absorbing material that is suitable for wheelchair use.

2. A universally designed playground should contain a wide variety of play opportunities that present a wide variety of challenges for all children. Play opportunities should include motor skills development (both large and fine muscle development), use of social skills, use of imagination, and places for dramatic play. Play opportunities should not focus solely on physical prowess or athletic ability, and of course, playground features should offer appropriate challenges for the intended user age group. Play challenges for toddlers are very different than those for school-age children.

3. The accessible route on a playground should reach those parts of the playground that contain play opportunities that are easiest to use and those features that are specifically intended to be accessible to children with mobility impairments, such as transfer points or wheelchair ramps. If an accessible route reaches an accessible equipment entrance such as a transfer point, which in turn provides access to a slide, then the accessible route should also meet the exit of the slide to provide a full accessible sliding loop. An accessible route should also connect to adjacent facilities such as parking areas or related buildings.

4. Keep in mind the range of abilities and disabilities and try to understand how to best meet the needs of the community that will be using the playground. Though a wheelchair is a typical icon for accessible features such as parking spaces and restrooms, it is by far not the most common assistive device in use. All children, especially those with visual or hearing impairments, will benefit from play opportunities that appeal to as many senses as possible. Include tactile and auditory activities if possible.

5. The playground should meet the needs of all users. It should provide an integrated setting where people of all abilities can play together. This basic intent of Universal Design is in direct contrast to the concept of separate-but-equal

facilities as may have been done in the past in those few playgrounds where any provision for accessibility was made at all. The goal of Universal Design on the playground is to provide a setting that allows for the "mainstreaming" of children with disabilities so that they can interact with their peers. Children with disabilities, when "mainstreamed," tend to grow and progress both physically and mentally whole while their able-bodied peers learn cooperation and openness to differences.

6. Finally, a playground of Universal Design can only be of benefit if it is safe. Always keep in mind current safety standards and guidelines. For a copy of the American Society of Testing and Materials (ASTM) standard F-1487 on "Playground Equipment for Public Use," contact ASTM, 100 Barr Harbor Drive, West Conshohocken, PA 19428, (610) 832-9585. For a copy of the Consumer Product Safety Commission's "Handbook for Public Playground Safety," write to U.S. Consumer Product Safety Commission, Washington, DC 20207.

CHAPTER 11

THE MULTI- AND PRINT MEDIA

PRINT PRINT PRINT PRINT PRINT

That's why the eye doctor uses that chart with different size letters.

When the concept of recordings for the blind was developed no one suspected it would turn into a multimillion dollar growth industry. But today, 50 years later, it is a multimillion dollar industry. As we enter a media revolution universally designed images become more and more important because we don't know who will be watching, reading, touching, or listening. In order to reach the widest possible audience, care, and an understanding of the parameters regarding visual expression and sound generation, will become extremely important. This chapter deals with those parameters and their effect on communication. Clarity and precision should be the watchwords of the media. The ability to clearly comprehend the meaning **and** the message will help everyone understand the media content better. Radio was a medium not intended for the blind but was designed from the beginning to compensate for the fact that all listeners could not **see** its content. So the actors, entertainers (including a ventriloquist!), moderators, news people, journalists, and storytellers had to paint verbal pictures that triggered the imagination.

Print Accessibility

When the purpose of a publication is to communicate information or ideas to a public, there are certain rules that will allow that publication to be more visually consumed. Because we have become a society in which instant communication is a given, many people will not take the time to decipher print communications that do not allow them instant access. A confusing flyer is instantly dropped on the sidewalk. A confusing ad in a magazine is ignored.

To make print media accessible and interesting requires intelligence, imagination, and creativity—three items always in short supply. Designers have said that it is an insult to their aesthetic sensibility when they must live within the guidelines of readability. The sonnet is a difficult, poetic form. This form never stopped Shakespeare from writing great sonnets, but few sonnets are written today. Perhaps it is because we have few poets who are as capable as Shakespeare in showing a full range of creativity within the tightly defined confines of this poetic form. Accessible design is not as nearly difficult as writing a sonnet. Perhaps if we had more poetic designers who understand this fact, we could accept the notion that what they create is art. And they could accept that they are not paid to do art, they are paid to create a vehicle to communicate, to inform, or to persuade.

There are more that 12 million Americans with a significant visual loss that cannot be substantially corrected. These people are not legally blind. Many of these people are not even aware that their eyesight is less than perfect. When you add to this population those people who simply do not have time to read difficult text, you have a sizable group of people.

Here are a few rules to allow people to see what you have to say.

1. **Contrast.** A black sans serif letter on a white background is the primary example of contrast. Studies made more than 30 years ago showed that Helvetica was the easiest-to-read typeface. Serif and script types are more difficult for everyone to read. The reason is simple to understand. As a typeface picks up the ornate appendages that define it as a serif type, it becomes more like a script type. The blending of lines in a script type are almost impossible to read for millions of Americans who are not considered to have a visual impairment.

   When screens and background art are laid over type they add to the difficulty of those who would easily read the print. Screens of greater than 20 percent reduce the contrast to the point where many people must concentrate to understand the written message.

   The color and texture of the paper can also reduce the contrast. Often designers will attempt to place a complementary ink color on the paper, such as a brown ink on a caramel-tone paper. The artistic statement is obvious, but too often the lack of contrast makes reading difficult.

   Surface glare is a difficult situation to balance. While the gloss of the paper can add to the contrast for many people, it can be difficult for others to read. The safest road is a nonglare surface with nonmetallic ink.

2. **Type size and spacing.** Attempting to pack as much information as possible into a small space can be as dangerous as trying to put too much space between your words, lines, and thoughts. A balance between the spaces between words and lines is a judgment call based on the amount of information you have to deliver and the amount of space into which you have to deliver the information. When you drop the type size below 10 point you begin to lose a sizable proportion of the American reading population.

3. **Field of vision and format.** The boundary of design will always be the format you are required to use. An 8½″ × 11″ magazine format provides you with the maximum parameters of space. However, your intelligence, imagination, and creativity determine how you will use that space. While three columns are generally the norm for such a format, one column, one and a half columns, and two or three columns are standard widths within that parameter. Column width should be dictated by readability. A line too short or too long is distracting.

When a graphic designer uses a client's work to make an artistic statement, that statement is quite often for the benefit of the designer, not the client. Being creative and imaginative does not preclude communications. Graphic designers are hired to **communicate,** not to create an entry into the next design competition.

George A. Covington
July 28, 1995
Copyrighted

Feature: Kodak Copier

Eastman Kodak Company's Office Imaging organization has an award-winning series of copiers that have been designed for universal access. The Kodak ImageSource 70 copier is available with an optional access kit that makes the copier-printer accessible to individuals who are seated or standing. The kit allows the feeder-scanner to be separated from the main operating unit and set on a separate table at a convenient level for both standing and seated users. (*Courtesy Eastman Kodak Company.*)

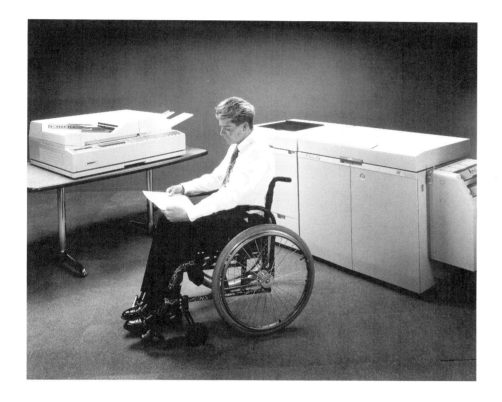

Figure 11.1 **Kodak Copier 1575.**

Product: Kodak Copier

The control panel can be easily accessed from the front of the machine and the open-feeder design is at chair height for easy access. Designers made loading paper and retrieving documents easier by placing paper supplies and exit trays at convenient work heights. In addition, designers made all doors and covers easily accessible by using push/pull latches that can be operated with a single hand. A unique clamshell design makes the entire paper path in the main operating unit accessible when the top cover is opened. (*Courtesy Eastman Kodak Company.*)

Figure 11.2 **Kodak Copier 1575.**

Product: Kodak Copier

Because the Kodak ImageSource 70 copier-printer can be networked, individuals can send their work directly to the unit from their computers without leaving their desk. Being able to load paper, run jobs, and even clear the ubiquitous copier jam, whether sitting or standing, really makes this machine a Universal Design milestone. (*Courtesy Eastman Kodak Company.*)

Figure 11.3 **Kodak Copier 1575.**

Figure 11.4 **Kodak Copier 1575.**

Product: Kodak Copier

Doug Beaudet, director of the ACCESS research program at Kodak's Human Factor Lab, worked closely with Kodak's copier customers and local disability groups to create a copier-printer that would serve the greatest number of people. Along the way, they broke a few rules and broke down a few barriers in the office environment. (*Courtesy Eastman Kodak Company.*)

Product: Books on Tape

Three thousand titles to listen to while commuting, exercising, or relaxing. Readers were, at one time, people who read for those who couldn't. Now there are also entertainers re-

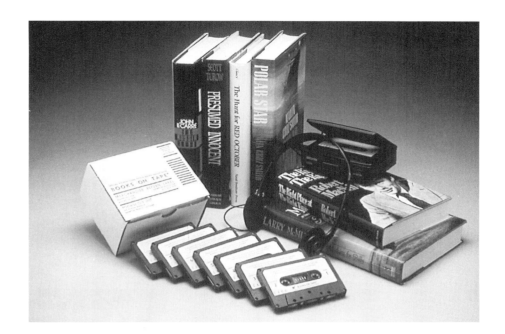

Figure 11.5 **Books On Tape.**

Figure 11.6 **Aladdin by TeleSensory.**

sponding to a mobile, inquisitive society. Wasting two hours commuting just isn't done—we are either on the phone or listening to tapes or discs. (*Courtesy of Books on Tape, P.O. Box 7900, Newport Beach, CA 92658–7900.*)

Product: Personal Reader Device

The Aladdin personal reader is a simple magnification device that lets you magnify up to 25 times whatever you want to read. If you can see large-print newspaper headlines Aladdin will probably work for you. (*Courtesy of TeleSensory.*)

Product: Personal Reader Device

The Aladdin personal reader is a simple magnification device that lets you read a letter, or . . . (*Courtesy of TeleSensory.*)

Figure 11.7 **Aladdin by TeleSensory.**

Figure 11.8 **Aladdin by TeleSensory.**

Figure 11.9 **Aladdin by TeleSensory.**

Figure 11.10 **Aladdin by TeleSensory.**

Product: Personal Reader Device
a cookbook, or . . . (*Courtesy of TeleSensory.*)

Product: Personal Reader Device
a prescription, or . . . (*Courtesy of TeleSensory.*)

Product: Personal Reader Device
read a book to your children. (*Courtesy of TeleSensory.*)

Figure 11.11 **Aladdin by TeleSensory.**

Product: Personal Reader Device
The Aladdin also lets you see your granddaughter's photo.
(*Courtesy of TeleSensory.*)

MULTI- AND PRINT MEDIA TRANSITIONS TO REMEMBER

Transitions from one space, service, or product to another often present barriers whether physical or psychological.

1. Reading Access

2. Copier Access

3. Accessibility

4. Lighting Access

CHECK LIST
Accessible Print

1. Use sans serif typefaces, such as Helvetica medium.

2. Avoid complicated images that overlap or are distorted.

3. Avoid large fields of red because some people, especially epileptics, react badly to red.

4. Yellow can be seen more easily than other colors.

5. Avoid multiple typefaces on a single page.

6. Sepia images are more easily seen than high-contrast black and white.

7. Avoid high-gloss papers; they reflect light and make reading more difficult.

8. Avoid harsh changes in font size.

9. Print on white or light gray backgrounds. Print that is of the same or similar value is difficult to see.

10. Avoid highly contrasting colors.

11. Use 14 point type.

CONCLUSION

We hope there isn't a conclusion to the proliferation of well-designed, universally accessible spaces, products, and services. We see evidence everyday that inclusiveness is epidemic. Seamlessness is replacing accessibility issues. Universal Design is on its way to being for the norm not for the exception. Inclusion is replacing exclusion. The concept of handicapped is replaced by abled access; access is replaced by integration. Wireless products, the Internet, the World Wide Web and other expansive, enabling services, free us from a skill-based society.

Thinking is our most important product. Enlightened thinking is our new and improved product. Enabling thinking is replacing skills as the major factor of success.

We have used every cliché to try and answer questions about accessibility, without apology. We are trying to fight fire with fire, so to speak, since most prejudices are bound up in clichés.

Universal Design is a goal, an ideal that everyone who designs, builds, and writes should have.

The next book is already in the works, since we can't keep up with the tidal wave of information generated about accessibility.

A UNIVERSAL DESIGN CHECKLIST
Transitions to Keep in Mind

1. RAMPS: Ramps are more universal than stairs.

2. CONTRAST: Use high contrast between surfaces.

3. LEVELS: Mark all level changes.

4. COMMON SENSES: Use all the senses *all* the time.

5. DOORS: Wide, open portals accept everyone.

6. REACH: Put everything within easy reach. Make it available.

7. SAFETY FIRST: Does a product prevent unintended and dangerous use?

8. USE: Imagine someone else is going to use, read, or work at or with, whatever you do. Does a product project an intuitive use?

9. LIGHT EVERYTHING: Good lighting is especially useful to show up contrasts, whether in color or textures, and provide a safer environment.

10. AGING IS A FACT OF LIFE: Remember people grow up and down. Their mobility, strength, and agility are lessened and must be accommodated. Their height is frequently reduced or compromised with arthritis and osteoporosis.

11. SMALL ADULTS AND BIG CHILDREN LIVE TOGETHER: Remember not all adults are big (see #10 above), and not all children are small.

12. USE COLOR: On faucets, for example, red is HOT and blue is COLD.

13. LEVERAGE: Leverage compensates for reduced strength, especially in gripping.

14. CONTEXT: Always design products for the context in which they will be used: office chairs in the office, fishing gear in a boat, etc. (The VCR was probably conceived in a brightly lit studio by able-bodied designers, not by visually impaired designers in a dimly lit room late at night.) Keep in mind that Universal Design does not necessarily mean a product can (or will) be used everywhere.

15. CORDLESSNESS: Cords tangle, limit use, and can cause accidents.

16. **DEXTERITY: Can product be used by everyone whether right or left handed?**

17. **DETAILS vs. DESIGN: If you can't reach the switch to turn it on, because it has been hidden (for aesthetic appeal), then the machine isn't very accessible. An ornately designed staircase looks lovely, but not if you're in a wheelchair. Universal Design is not about what something looks like but about what it can do—for someone.**

APPENDIX

Professional Organizations

AAF
American Architectural Foundation
American Institute of Architects
1735 New York Avenue
Washington, DC 20006
202-626-7568

ACD
American Center for Design
233 East Ontario, Suite 500
Chicago, IL 60611
312-787-2018

ADPSR
American Designers & Planners for Social
    Responsibility
175 Fifth Avenue, Suite 2210
New York, NY 10010

AIA
American Institute of Architects
1735 New York Avenue, NW
Washington, DC 20006
202-626-7310

AIGA
American Institute of Graphic Design
164 Fifth Avenue
New York, NY 10011
212-807-1799

APDF
Association of Professional Design Firms
1 Story Street
Cambridge, MA 02138
617-864-7474

ASA
American Society on Aging
833 Market Street, Suite 511
San Francisco, CA 94103
415-974-9600
415-974-0300 FAX

ASID
American Society of Interior Designers
608 Massachusetts Avenue
Washington, DC 20002
202-546-3480

ASLA
American Society of Landscape Architects
4401 Connecticut Avenue
Washington, DC 20008
202-686-2752

BFD
Barrier Free Design
2075 Bayview Avenue
Toronto M4N 3M5
Canada
416-480-6000

BIFMA
Business Institute of Furniture Manufacture
2680 Horizon Dr SE, Suite A1
Grand Rapids, MI 49546
616-285-3963

CRAB
Chesapeak Region Accessible Boating
P.O. Box 6564
Annapolis, MD 21401-0564
410-974-2628

DI
Design Exchange
P.O. Box 18
Toronto-Dominion Centre
Toronto M5K 1B2
Canada
416-363-6141

DMI
Design Management Institute
20 Park Plaza #321
Boston, MA 02116
617-350-7097

HAI
Hospital Audiences Inc.
220 West 42nd Street, 13th Floor
New York, NY 10109-0197
212-687-1960

Human Factors & Ergonomics Society
P.O. Box 1369
Santa Monica, CA 90406-1369
310-394-1811
310-394-2410 FAX

IBD
Institute of Business Designers
Merchandise Mart
Chicago, IL 60654
312-467-1950

ICSID
International Council of Societies of Industrial
    Design
Yrjonkatu 11E
00120 Helsinki, Finland
358-060-7611

IDSA
Industrial Design Society of America
1142 East Walker Road
Great Falls, VA 22066
703-759-0100

IFMA
International Facility Management Association
International Headquarters
1 East Greenway, Suite 1100
Houston, TX 77046-0194
713-622-6515

NEA
National Endowment for the Arts
1100 Pennsylvania Avenue NW
Washington, DC 20506
202-685-5437

NHBA
National Home Builders Association
Washington, DC 20005
202-822-0200

NKBA
National Kitchen & Bath Association
67 Willow Grove Street
Hackettstown, NJ 07840
908-852-0033

OBD
Organization of Black Designers
300 M Street SW, Suite N110
Washington, DC 20034
202-659-3918

PDCI
Package Design Council International
481 Carlisle Drive
Herndon, VA 22070
703-318-7225

RSA
Jane Saks Cohen
The Royal Society for the Encouragement of
Arts, Manufacture & Commerce
8 John Adam Street
London, WC2N 6EZ
England
0171-930-5115
0171-839-5805 FAX

SEGD
Society of Environmental Graphic Designers
1 Story Street
Cambridge, MA 02138
617-868-3381

SND
The Society of Newspaper Design
Box 179292 Dulles International Airport
Washington, DC 20041
703-620-1083

VIA
Valorization De L'innovation dans
    L'ameublement
4-6-8 Cour De Commerce Saint Andre
Paris 75006
France
43 29 39 36

BIBLIOGRAPHY

Access for All: A Guide for People with Disabilities to New York City Cultural Institutions. Hospital Audiences, Inc. and WCBS-AM News-Radio 88, 220 West 42nd St., 13th floor, New York, NY 10036. 1992.

Access to Mass Transit for Blind and Visually Impaired Travellers. Mark M. Uslan, et. al., eds. New York: American Foundation for the Blind.

The Accessibility Checklist. Susan Goltsman, Timothy Gilbert, and Steven Wohlford. 2d ed. 1993.

Accessible Design for Hospitality. Thomas D. Daves Jr. and Kim A. Beasley. Paradigm Design Group. 2d ed., McGraw-Hill.

Accessible Design of Consumer Products. Trade Research and Development Center, Consumer Guidelines Project, S-151 Waisman Center, University of Wisconsin, 1500 Highland Avenue, Madison, WI 53705. ($15.00 + $10.00 handling.)

Accessible Environments: Toward Universal Design. Ron Mace. North Carolina State University, Center for Accessible Housing, Box 8613, Raleigh, NC 27695-8613. 1989. ($3.50)

Achieving Physical and Communication Accessibility. Adaptive Environments Center, 374 Congress Street, Suite 301, Boston, MA 02210, 617-695-1225, Fax 617-482-8099. ($25.00)

Action on Accessibility: Proceedings of the International Accessibility MiniSummit. Center for Accessible Housing, North Carolina State University, Box 8613, Raleigh, NC 27695, 919-515-3082, Fax 919-515-3023. ($4.50)

Adaptable Housing: Marketing Accessible Housing for Everyone. U.S. Department of Housing and Urban Development, P.O. Box 6091, Rockville, MD 20850, 301-251-5154, 800-245-2691. ($4.00)

The Americans with Disabilities Act: Accessibility Guidelines for Buildings and Facilities, Transportation Facilities, Transportation Vehicles. U.S. Architectural and Transportation Barriers Compliance Board (USATBCB), Suite 1000, 1331 F Street NW, Washington, DC 20004-1111, 1992.

The American with Disabilities Act: Title II Technical Assistance Manual. Public Access Section, Civil Rights Division, U.S. Department of Justice,

P.O. Box 66738, Washington, DC 20035–6738, 202–514–0301.

The American with Disabilities Act: Title III Technical Assistance Manual. Public Access Section, Civil Rights Division, U.S. Department of Justice, P.O. Box 66738, Washington, DC 20035–6738, 202–514–0301. 1992.

Anthropometric Methods: Designing to Fit the Human Body. John A. Roebuck. Human Factors & Ergonomic Society, P.O. Box 1369, Santa Monica, CA 90406–1369.

Applying Technology in the Work Environment. Arkansas Research and Training Center, Media and Publications Section, P.O. Box 1358, Hot Springs, AR 71902, 501–624–4411. 1990. ($13.00)

Arkitekten (journal, various articles on universal design). Arkitektens Forlag, Nyhavn 43, 1051 Kobenhavn K, Copenhagen, Denmark.

Assistive Technology and the Americans with Disabilities Act. STAR Program, 300 Centennial Building, 658 Cedar Street, St. Paul, MN 55155, 612–296–2771. (Pamphlet.)

Assistive Technology and Home Modifications for Individuals with Disabilities. STAR Program, 300 Centennial Building, 658 Cedar Street, St. Paul, MN 55155, 612–296–2771. (Pamphlet.)

Assistive Technology and Older Minnesotans. STAR Program, 300 Centennial Building, 658 Cedar Street, St. Paul, MN 55155, 612–296–2771. (Pamphlet.)

Assistive Technology and the Workplace. STAR Program, 300 Centennial Building, 658 Cedar Street, St. Paul, MN 55155, 612–296–2771. (Pamphlet.)

Barrier-Free Design: Selected New York State Laws and Code Provisions. Eastern Paralyzed Veterans Association. November 1992, revised.

Barrier-Free Design: The Law, Vol. 1. Text by Terence J. Moakley and Richard D. McDonald, Eastern Paralyzed Veterans Association, Barrier-Free Design Dept., Jackson Heights, NY: EPVA, 1989, 718–803–EPVA.

"Barrier-Free" NoShohin-Kaihatsu. (The development of Barrier-Free Design.) E&C Project Nihon Keizai Shimbun, Inc. Tokyo, Japan.

The Bathroom. (Unique research on bathrooms.) Alexander Kira, various editions.

Beautiful Barrier-Free: A Visual Guide to Accessibility. Cynthia Leibrock with Susan Behar. New York: Van Nostrand Reinhold. 1993. 720.42 G229.

Benefits of Accessory Unit Housing for Elderly Persons and Persons with Disabilities, CAH Fact Sheet. Center for Accessible Housing, North Carolina State University, Box 8613, Raleigh, NC 27695, 919–515–3082, Fax 919–515–3023. ($1.00)

Building Design for Handicapped and Aged Persons. Gilda M. Haber and Thomas Blank. New York: Council on Tall Buildings and Urban Habitat, Committee 56, and McGraw–Hill. 1947. 720.42 B932.

The Complete Guide to Barrier-Free Housing: Convenient Living for the Elderly and Physically Handicapped. Gary D. Branson and Hilary W. Swinson, eds. White Hall, VA: Betterway Publications, 1991. 720.42 B821.

Consumer Products and Individuals with Disabilities. STAR Program, 300 Centennial Building, 658 Cedar Street, St. Paul, MN 55155, 612–296–2771. (Pamphlet.)

A Consumer's Guide to Home Adaptation. Center for Accessible Housing, North Carolina State University, Box 8613, Raleigh, NC 27695, 919–515–3082, Fax 919–515–3023. ($9.50)

Creating an Accessible Campus. Maggie Coons and Margaret Milner, eds. Washington, DC: Association of Physical Plant Administrators of Universities and Colleges. 1978. 720.42 C912.

Design for Accessibility. Robert James Sorenson. New York: McGraw–Hill. 1979. 720.42 S713.

Design for Dignity: Accessible Environments for People with Disabilities. William Lebovich. New York: John Wiley & Sons. 1993.

Design for Hospitality: Planning for Accessible Hotels and Motels. Thomas D. Davies and Kim A. Beasley. New York: Nichols Publishing. 1988.

Design for Independent Living: Housing Accessibility Institute Resource Book. Center for Accessible Housing, North Carolina State University, Box 8613, Raleigh, NC 27695, 919–515–3082, Fax 919–515–3023. ($50.00)

Design for Physical Independence Program, Industrial Design Curriculum Development. Robert Anders and Daniel Fechtner. Industrial Design Dept., School of Art & Design, Pratt Institute, New York. 1992.

Design in Finland 1989. (journal, special issue of Finnish Trade Review.) Finnish Foreign Trade Assn. (F.F.T.A.), P.O. Box 908, Arkadiankatu 4–6 B, SF–00101, Helsinki, Finland. 1989.

Design in Use. Bahco Products, brochure. Ergonomi Design Gruppen (EDG), Box 140 21, Missionsvagen 24, S–161 14, Bromma, Stockholm, 46–8–26 25 25.

Design Primer: Drawing Design. Frederick Blumlein. Industrial Design Dept., School of Art & Design, and Pratt Center for Advanced Design Research (CADRE), Pratt Institute, New York. 1993.

Design Primer: Universal Design. Industrial Design Dept., School of Art & Design, and Pratt Center for Advanced Design Research (CADRE), Pratt Institute, New York. 1992. ($18.00)

Designing Environments for Handicapped Children: A Design Guide and Case Study. Education Facilities Laboratories, NY. 1979. 720.42 D457

Designs for Independent Living. Raymond Lifchez. Berkeley, CA: University of California Press.

Directory of Accessible Building Products: Products Making Houses User Friendly for Everyone. NAHB Research Center, NAHB Research Center, 400 Prince George's Blvd., Upper Marlboro, MD 20772–8731, 301–249–4000. 1993.

The Do-Able Renewable Home: Making Your Home Fit Your Needs. American Association of Retired Persons, P.O. Box 22796, Long Beach, CA 90801–5796. 1992.

Extend Their Reach. Electronic Industries Association, 2001 Pennsylvania Avenue, Washington, DC 20006, 202–457–8705. 1992. (Section on vision impairments is available on audiocassette.) (Pamphlet.)

Fair Housing Amendments Act Accessibility Guidelines Slide Show. Center for Accessible Housing, North Carolina State University, Box 8613, Raleigh, NC 27695, 919–515–3082, Fax 919–515–3023. ($150.00 or $75.00 nonprofit)

Fair Housing Amendments Act: Design Requirements Questions and Answers, CAH Fact Sheet. Center for Accessible Housing, North Carolina State University, Box 8613, Raleigh, NC 27695, 919–515–3082, Fax 919–515–3023. ($1.00)

Fair Housing Amendments Act: Provisions Relating to Discrimination Based on Disability, CAH Fact Sheet. Center for Accessible Housing, North Carolina State University, Box 8613, Raleigh, NC 27695, 919–515–3082, Fax 919–515–3023. ($1.00)

Fair Housing Amendments Act: Reasonable
Modification of Existing Premises, CAH
Fact Sheet. Center for Accessible Housing,
North Carolina State University, Box 8613,
Raleigh, NC 27695, 919-515-3082, Fax
919-515-3023. ($1.00)

Fair Housing Amendments Act: Substantial
Equivalency, CAH Fact Sheet. Center for
Accessible Housing, North Carolina State
University, Box 8613, Raleigh, NC 27695,
919-515-3082, Fax 919-515-3023.
($1.00)

Fair Housing Design Guide for Accessibility.
Thomas D. Daves Jr. and Kim A. Beasley.
Paradigm Design Group, 801 18th Street
NW Washington, D. C., 20006,
202-416-7645, Fax 202-4416-7647.
($49.95)

Federal Accessibility Standards: General Services
Administration, Dept. of Defense, Dept. of
Housing and Urban Development, Postal
Service. Architectural and Transportation
Compliance Board, U.S. Government,
Washington, DC. 1985.

Financing Accessibility Modifications, CAH Fact
Sheet. Center for Accessible Housing, North
Carolina State University, Box 8613,
Raleigh, NC 27695, 919-515-3082, Fax
919-515-3023. ($1.00)

For Convenience Sake. For Convenience Sake
Co., 4092B Howard Avenue, Kensington,
MD 20895. (Catalog.)

Getting in Touch with Play. Kim Blakley, Mary
Ann Long, Roger Hart. The Lighthouse Inc.
($8.00)

Handicapped at Home. Sydney Foot. Design
Councill, 28 Haymarket, London, SW1
Y4SU. 1977.

Home Financing for Older People, CAH Fact
Sheet. Center for Accessible Housing, North
Carolina State University, Box 8613,
Raleigh, NC 27695, 919-515-3082, Fax
919-515-3023. ($1.00)

Hospitable Design for Healthcare and Senior
Communities. Albert Bush-Brown. New
York: Van Nostrand Reinhold. 1992.

Hospital Interior Architecture: Creating Healing
Environments for Special Patient
Populations. Jain Maekui. New York: Van
Nostrand Reinhold. 1992.

The Housemate Agreement, CAH Tech Pack
(TP). Center for Accessible Housing, North
Carolina State University, Box 8613,
Raleigh, NC 27695, 919-515-3082, Fax
919-515-3023. ($3.00)

Housing Adaptations for Disabled People.
Research for the Disabled Living
Foundation, Terence Lockhart. New York:
The Architectural Press. 1981.

Housing Definitions: Accessible, Adaptable, and
Universal Design, CAH Fact Sheet. Center
for Accessible Housing, North Carolina
State University, Box 8613, Raleigh, NC
27695, 919-515-3082, Fax 919-515-3023.
($1.00)

Housing for the Life Span of All People. Ronald
Mace, U.S. Dept. of Housing and Urban
Development, HUD User, P.O. Box 6091,
Rockville, MD 20850, 301-251-5154.
(Pamphlet, $5.00)

Housing Interiors for the Disabled and Elderly.
Betty Ann Boetticher Raschko. New York:
Van Nostrand Reinhold. 1982, 1991.

Human Factors and Industrial Design in
Consumer Products. (Proceedings of a
symposium). Dept. of Engineering, Tufts
University, May, 1980.

Humanscale. Niels Diffrient, Alvin R. Tilley,
David Harman, and Joan C. Bardagly.
(Series of nine adjustable templates.) New
York: Henry Dreyfuss Associates, and
Cambridge, MA: MIT Press, 1978 to
present editions.

Ideas for Making Your Home Accessible. Betty
Garce. Bloomington, IL: Accent Press,
1979.

Ifo Bathroom. Ifo Sanitar Ab. Box 140, S-295 22, Bromoila, Sweden, 46-0-456-480-99. (Brochure.)

Interior Design. (Journal, special issue on universal design.) Vol. 63, no. 11 (August 1992). Newton, MA: Cahners Publishing. 1992.

Journal of Visual Impairment and Blindness. American Foundation for the Blind.

Kitchen and Bath Design News Magazine, PTN Publishing Co., 445 Broad Hollow Road Melville, NY 11747. 516-845-2700.

The Lighthouse. (Journal.) The Lighthouse, eds.

Making Physical Education and Recreation Facilities Accessible to All. Information and Research Utilization Center in Physical Education and Recreation for the Handicapped. Washington, DC: American Alliance for Health, Physical Education and Recreation. 1977.

Managing Information Resources for Accessibility. General Services Administration, Reference Center, Information Resource Management Service, Room 3227, Washington, DC 20405, 202-501-4906.

Maxiaids. (Catalog.) Maxiaids, P.O. Box 3209, Farmingdale, NY 11735.

MoMA Catalog, Winter 1993–94. "Universal Design for Independent Living." Museum of Modern Art, coordinated by Marsha Armitage, NY: MoMA, Mail Order Dept., 11 West 53rd St., New York, NY 10019-5401, 212-708-9888, 800-447-6662.

MoMA Catalog, Fall 1992, "Designs for Independent Living." Museum of Modern Art, coordinated by Marsha Armitage, NY: MoMA, Mail Order Dept., 11 West 53rd St., New York, NY 10019-5401, 212-708-9888, 800-447-6662.

The New ADA: Compliance and Costs. Deborah S. Kearney. R.S. Means Co., Inc., Construction Publishers and Consultants, 100 Construction Plaza, P.O. Box 800, Kingston, MA 02364-0800, 617-585-7880, 1992

New Households, New Housing. Karen Franck, ed. New York: Van Nostrand Reinhold. 1991.

Opening All Doors, ADA: A Resource Guide. American Institute of Architects, 1735 New York Ave NW, Washington, DC 20006-5292, 202-626-7300.

Parenting Plus—Raising Children with Special Needs. Peggy Finston, M.D. Hastings-On-Hudson, NY: T.F.S.C.—Enabling Devices Inc. Various editions.

Perfectly Safe (The Catalog for Parents Who Care). Perfectly Safe, 7245 Whipple Ave., NW, North Canton, OH 44720. 330-966-5069.

Performance Design of Safer Windows. Michael Bill, et al. Research for U.S. Consumer Product Safety Commission, Special Engineering Studies Division, Buffalo, NY: BOSTI Inc. 1977.

Personal Computers and Special Needs. Frank G. Bowe. SYBEX, 2344 Sixth St., Berkeley, CA 94710. 1984.

The Planner's Guide to Barrier Free Meeting. Barrier Free Environments Inc., P.O. Box 30634, Raleigh, NC 27622.

Precedence, Bathtub for Wheelchair Access. Kohler Co., Audio-Visual Dept., Kohler, WI 53044, 414-457-4441. (Brochure and videotape.)

Preserving the Past and Making It Accessible for People with Disabilities. National Park Service, Preservation Assistance Division, P.O. Box 37127, Washington, DC, 202-343-9578. (Pamphlet.)

Proceedings: 1992 IDSA Educators Conference. Industrial Design Society of America, 1142 E. Walker Road, Great Falls, VA 22066, 703-759-0100. ($20.00)

Proposal for a Solution: Nordic Cooperation on Technical Aids and Disability. Lars Ege and

Mogens Wiederholt, eds. The Nordic Committee on Disability, Box 510, S-162 15, Vallingby, Sweden, 46-8-620-18-90, Fax 46-8-739-24-00. (Brochure.)

Rehab Brief: Design for the Life Span of All People. Vol. 10, no. 12 (1987). National Rehabilitation Information Center (NARIC), 8455 Colesville Road, Suite 935, Silver Springs, MD 20910-3319, 301-588-9284.

Rethinking Architecture: Design Students and Physically Disabled People. Raymond Lifchez. Berkeley, CA: University of California Press. 1987, 1993 (Also available in videotape.)

RFB Issues. (Newsletter) Vol. 37, no. 3 (Fall, Winter 1992). Recording for the Blind, 20 Roszel Road, Princeton, NJ 08540, 609-452-0606

Rolli Moden Stora Katalogen. Rolli Combino AB, Box 1146, S-43623, Askim, Sweden, 031-681005, Fax 031-280463. (Catalog in Swedish.)

Specially Adapted and Individually Made Aids for Children. Stig Persson and Bengt Gustafsson, eds. International Commission on Technical Aids Housing and Transportation, ICTA Information Center, Box 510, S-162 15, Vallingby, Sweden, J46-8-620-17-00. January, 1982.

Tactile Graphics. Polly K. Edman. American Foundation for the Blind, 15 West 16th Street, New York, NY 10011. 1992.

Technical Paper on Accessibility Codes and Standards. The U.S. Access Board, 1331 F Street NW, Suite 1000, Washington, DC 20004, 202-272-5434. 1989.

Toys for Special Children. (Catalog, Vol. 3, no. 4 (1993)). T.F.S.C.—Enabling Devices Inc., 385 Warburton Ave., Hastings-On-Hudson, NY 10706, 914-478-0960, 800-832-8697.

Understanding the Americans with Disabilities Act. Eastern Paralyzed Veterans Association, 75-20 Astoria Blvd., Jackson Heights, NY, 11370-1177, 1991, 718-803-EPVA.

U.F.A.S. Retrofit Guide. (Accessibility modifications for existing buildings designed to be used in conjunction with the ADA.) Barrier Free Environments Inc., PO Box 30634, Raleigh, NC 27622. Van Nostrand Reinhold. (pub). 1993.

Universal Access to Outdoor Recreation: A Design Guide. U.S.D.A. Forest Service, and PLAE, Inc., Washington, DC. 1993.

Universal Design Newsletter. John P.S. Salmen, ed. Universal Designers & Consultants, Inc., 1700 Rockville Pike, Suite 110, Rockville, MD 20852-9639, 301-770-7890, Fax 301-770-4338

Vardags VARA. (Catalog) Konsumentverlet, Box 503, 162 15, Vallingby, Sweden, 08-759-83-00. 1992.

The Workplace Workbook: An Illustrated Guide to Job Accommodation and Assistive Technology. James Mueller. Washington, DC: The Dole Foundation. 1990.

The Workplace Workbook 2.0. James Mueller. Human Resources Development Press, 22 Amherst Road, Amherst, MA 01002, 800-822-2801. ($49.95)

VIDEOCASSETTES

About the ADA. 15 min. George Cochran, Dir. of PR, Eastern Paralyzed Veterans Association (EPVA), 75-20 Astoria Blvd., Jackson Heights, NY 11370-1177, 718-803-3782, Fax 718-803-0414.

Accessibility. 30 min. Terence Moakley, Asst. Dir. for Communications, EPVA, 75-20 Astoria Blvd., Jackson Heights, NY 11370-1177, 718-803-3782.

Accessible Design #32 & #33. 20 min. U.S. Architecture and Transportation, Barriers and Compliance Board, GSA, Washington, DC, 800-USA-ABLE.

The Accessible Place of Business. 30 min. John Salmen. Universal Designers & Con., 1700 Rockville Pike, Suite 110, Rockville, MD 20852, 301-770-7890. ($98.00)

Accessible Workstation. 7 min. Benson Kravtin, 39 Sidney Place, Brooklyn, NY 11201, 718-596-3916. ($15.00)

ADA Facts & Fears. 42 min. Cynthia Kay/Wayne Glatz Film & Video Inc., 214 E. Fulton St., Grand Rapids, MI, 616-776-0354.

Artist Milda Visbar '92–'93. 60 min. 92 Muscular Dystrophy Telethon and profile piece for new MDA document, Milda Visbar, New York, NY, 212-675-6293.

A Better Grip on Every Day Life. 9 min. Banvall and Lundberg, RFSU Rehab. Corp., I.D.E. Film, Stockholm, Sweden, Available from ETAC, USA Inc., 2325 Parklawn Drive, Suite P, Waukesha, IL 53186, 414-796-4600. (Free)

Building and Remodeling for Accessibility, 25 min. Home Time, 4275 Norex Drive, Chaska, MN 55318, 616-448-3812. (11.95 + $3.00 S/H)

"Callahan" The Story of John Callahan, Cartoonist. 9 min. Morley Safer, *60 Minutes,* CBS Inc., New York, NY 10019 800-848-3256, Ambrose Video Publishers Inc., 800-843-0048.

Designing for Accessibility, Beyond the ADA. 13 min. Herman Miller Inc., 855 E Main St. Zeeland, MI, 616-654-3676.

Designing For Health. 12:55 min. Beth Israel Hospital, Boston, MA 02215. Funding by Herman Miller. 617-667-8000.

Easy Access National Parks. 30 min. "Easy Access Challenge," Wendy Roth and Michael Tompane, 3456 Greenfield Avenue, Los Angeles, CA 90034, 310-559-3810.

"Entrances To The Past" Accessibility and Historic Preservation. $13.00, 28:25 min.,

National Parks Service, Historic Windsor, Inc., PO Box 1777, Windsor, VT 05089-0021, 802-674-6752. ($13.00)

Furnishings for the Physically Handicapped. 20 min. Deborah Kearney. Work Stations Inc., 165 Front Street, Chicopee, MA 01013, 413-598-8394.

The Hartford House. 28 min. Beverly Hynes Grace. IIT Hartford, 200 Executive Way, Southington, CT 06489, 203-547-5000.

A House for Someone Unlike Me. 40 min. Universal Design Education Project, College of Environmental Design, University of California, Berkeley, CA.

Innovation "The Future is Now." 57:36 min. Program 201. "Taking Care of Business." Program 202. "Home Sweet Home." Program 203. "The New ABCs." Transcript, WNET New York, NY: Innovation, PO Box 12361, Overland Park, KS 66212, 913-649-6381.

It's All In The Planning. 10 min. Carolyn Verweyst/Cynita Garrett. Whirlpool, 2000 M-63, Benton Harbor, MI 49022, 616-923-3164.

Opening Doors. 10 min. Opening Doors, Bill and Cheryl Duke, 8049 Ormesby, Woodford, VA 22580, 804-633-6752. (Sampler, $89.00)

Posturemate. 10 min. Electronic Variable Height Desk, 139 Burke Lane, Kneeland, CA 95549, 707-445-4841.

Precedence—A Bathtub for Wheelchair Access. 6:10 min. Kohler, Audio Visual Dept., Kohler, WI 53044, 414-457-4441. (Brochure and videotape)

Presalit Products for Am. Std. 120 min. Dick Zabella. American Standard, One Centennial Plaza, P.O. Box 6820, Piscataway, NJ 08855-6820, 908-980-3129.

Rethinking Architecture: Design Students and Physically Disabled People. Raymond Lifchez. Berkeley, CA: University of California Press. 1987, 1993 (Also available in print)

RFSU Grooming Video. 9 min. Banvall and Lundberg. RFSU Rehab. Corp., I.D.E. Film, Stockholm, Sweden, Available from ETAC USA Inc., 2325 Parklawn Drive, Suite P, Waukesha, IL 53186, 414-796-4600.

Toward Universal Design. 15 min. The Assistive Technology Program, National Rehab. Hospital, 102 Irving St. NW, Washington, DC; James Mueller, The UD Design Initiative, 4717 Wallney Knoll Court, Chantilly, VA 22021.

Understanding ANSI. 24 min. Victor Duncan Inc. 11 W. 42nd St. New York, NY 10036 212-642-4900 ($16.00)

Universal Design—A Design for All People. 10 min. American Society of Interior Designers, National Headquarters, 608 Massachusetts Avenue, Washington, DC 20002-6006, 202-546-3480. ($25.00)

Universal Design Kitchen. 5 min. Carolyn Verweyst and Cynita Garrett. Whirlpool, 2000 M-63, Benton Harbor, MI 49022, 616-923-3164.

Universal Design Kitchen. (Student thesis) Pratt Institute, J. Gikow 329 E. 83rd New York NY, 10028 212-758-7700

Work in Progress. 26 min. Ron Mace, Barrier Free Environments, P.O. Box 30634, Raleigh, NC 27622, 919-782-7823. ($17.98)

OTHER MEDIA AND SERVICES

The American Sign Language Dictionary on CD-
ROM. Martin L.A. Sternberg. New York:
Harper Collins, 800-424-6234.
CAH Selected Readings List. Center for
Accessible Housing, North Carolina State
University, Box 8613, Raleigh, NC 27695,
919-515-3082, Fax 919-515-3023.
($3.00)
National Support Center for Persons with
Disabilities. IBM. P.O. Box 8613, Atlanta,
GA 30301-2150, 800-426-2133. (Various
resources and publications available)

INDEX